Submarines!

Other Piccolo True Adventures

Aidan Chambers
Haunted Houses
More Haunted Houses
Great British Ghosts
Great Ghosts of the World

Richard Garrett
Hoaxes and Swindles
True Tales of Detection
Narrow Squeaks!
Great Sea Mysteries

Frank Hatherley
Bushrangers Bold!

Marie Herbert
Great Polar Adventures

Carey Miller
Airships and Balloons

Nicholas Monsarrat
The Boys' Book of the Sea

Sorche Nic Leodhas
Scottish Ghosts

Piccolo True Adventures

SUBMARINES!

Illustrations by David Till

Carey Miller

A Piccolo Original
Pan Books London and Sydney

First published 1971 by Pan Books Ltd,
Cavaye Place, London SW10 9PG
3rd printing 1976
© Carey Miller 1971
Illustrations © David Till 1971
ISBN 0 330 02829 4
Made and printed in Great Britain by
Cox & Wyman Ltd, London, Reading and Fakenham

CONTENTS

Chapter 1

The Invention of the Submarine

This is a book of submarine stories, and perhaps one of the very best stories of all is how the submarine came to be invented. For centuries men dreamed of a warship which would be 'invisible', which would travel underneath the surface of the sea and be able to take the enemy completely by surprise. But the dream proved very difficult to put into practice. It took a long time to develop the idea of the submarine, and many dangerous, tragic and sometimes funny things happened on the way.

The First Submarines

As far back as 332 BC there are stories about vessels that descended below the sea, but it is not until the sixteenth century AD that we have proper records of them. In the 200 years before 1775 we have accounts of seventeen submarine inventions, none of which worked properly. Probably they were more dangerous to the crew than to the enemy! The first workable models began to be developed towards the end of the eighteenth century.

*   *   *

Turtle

A young American student named David Bushnell found a way of making gunpowder explode under water. At the time of his discovery the Americans were fighting the British in the American War of Independence (1775–83) and New York Harbour was full of British warships. Bushnell needed some sort of underwater vessel to carry his bombs to their target so he decided to build one. This amazing invention was called the *Turtle*.

The *Turtle* was a wooden egg 7 feet deep by 5½ feet wide. It was so named because it looked like two turtle shells fastened together. It had a watertight hatch at the top and three small glass windows.

There was room for only one man inside and he was kept pretty busy! To submerge the boat he had to flood a water tank by opening a valve with his foot, and to rise to the surface again he had to push the water out of the tank by hand with a forcing pump. To move forwards he turned a handle revolving a propeller. At the same time he had to guide the boat by means of a tiller, while peering all the time through a tiny porthole.

The mine was fastened to the rear of the *Turtle*. It had a gunpowder charge, a 30-minute clockwork fuse, and was attached to a spike so that it could be driven into the hull of enemy ships.

A man named Sargeant Ezra Lee was chosen for the first risky underwater mission. He set off in the early hours of the morning, and all went well to begin with. Lee managed to guide his little contraption right underneath the hull of the British ship *Eagle* but then he came up against a snag. Bushnell had overlooked the fact that the bottom of the British ship had a copper coating as a

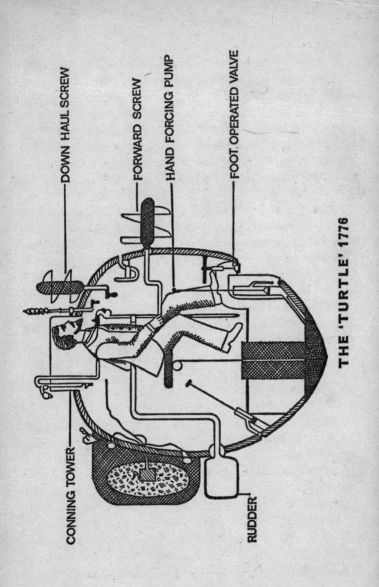

THE 'TURTLE' 1776

DOWN HAUL SCREW

FORWARD SCREW

HAND FORCING PUMP

FOOT OPERATED VALVE

CONNING TOWER

RUDDER

protection against underwater worms. Lee found it impossible to push his spike into the copper and after trying for some time decided to give up and make for the friendly shore.

He had to surface to see where he was going, and as by now it was growing light, his strange craft was spotted by some British soldiers who jumped into a rowing boat and gave chase. Lee was still carrying the heavy mine and in order to get up a bit more speed, he dropped it into the water. The soldiers, seeing this suspicious-looking object bobbing towards them, wisely gave up the chase. Thirty minutes later the mine exploded in the harbour, doing no damage to ships, but throwing enough water into the air to frighten away the British Fleet who moved off to a quieter anchorage.

A further attempt was made against a British ship, HMS *Cerberus*, but this was also unsuccessful and David Bushnell was forced through lack of money and government help to give up his experiments.

Nautilus

Twenty years later another American, Robert Fulton, designed a new version of the submarine. The War of Independence was over and the Americans were no longer interested in underwater weapons, so Fulton tried to sell the designs for his 'plunging boat' in Europe. In 1800 Napoleon Bonaparte, who was then ruler of France, became interested in the idea and granted Fulton enough money to go ahead with the building of his submarine, the *Nautilus*.

The hull was cigar-shaped and measured 21 feet 4 inches long by 5 feet wide. It was intended for a crew of three. The framework was iron, sheathed in copper, and

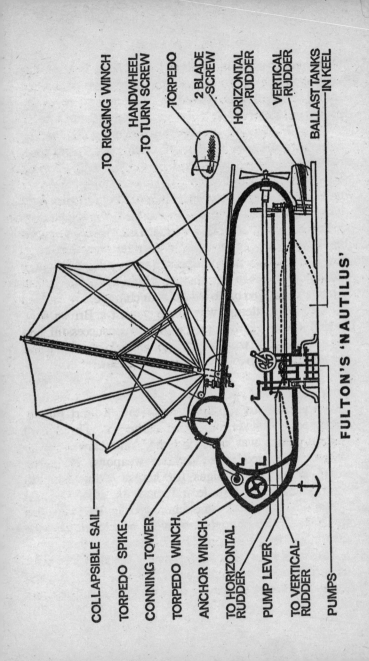

COLLAPSIBLE SAIL

TORPEDO SPIKE

CONNING TOWER

TORPEDO WINCH

ANCHOR WINCH

TO HORIZONTAL RUDDER

PUMP LEVER

TO VERTICAL RUDDER

PUMPS

TO RIGGING WINCH

HANDWHEEL TO TURN SCREW

TORPEDO

2 BLADE SCREW

HORIZONTAL RUDDER

VERTICAL RUDDER

BALLAST TANKS IN KEEL

FULTON'S 'NAUTILUS'

was strong enough to submerge to 20 feet. In the bow there was an entrance dome with a porthole for under-water viewing (rather similar to the conning towers we see on more modern submarines). In an attempt to dis-guise the *Nautilus* as some sort of surface craft, Fulton added a mast, which folded up like part of an umbrella, with a small sail.

The first trials, watched with interest by Napoleon, took place on the River Seine in 1801. Fulton, with two others, filled the ballast tanks and took the submarine down to 25 feet. They stayed there for twenty minutes being gradually pulled by the strong current towards the sea. Then, by hard cranking on the propeller, they sur-faced and came back at two knots. Napoleon now wished to see how the *Nautilus* would fare at sea, and he allowed Fulton a little more money – enough to pay for thick glass windows so that the submarine would not need candles which used up precious oxygen. At the same time a round tank filled with compressed air was fitted, which allowed the ship to stay down for as long as four hours. With money from his own pocket, Fulton then had the *Nautilus* transported to Brest Harbour to undergo sea trials.

Fulton had also invented a new type of explosive, similar to the one devised earlier by Bushnell. He called it a torpedo, after the electric ray fish that shocks his prey to death. He also intended to test this at Brest.

An old schooner, anchored off the coast, was the target for Fulton's latest invention. The *Nautilus*, with Fulton in control, approached, submerged, fixed the ex-plosive charge and successfully blew the ship into very small pieces.

Napoleon was quite excited. This would be the ideal

weapon for a sneak attack on the British Fleet! Many
French scientists agreed with him and were keen to give
Fulton enough money to build a full-size submarine, but
Napoleon's admirals were not too enthusiastic. Although amazed by the cleverness of the invention, they
thought that to use what they called an 'armed fish-boat'
would be as dishonourable as shooting someone in the
back.

Whilst the military men were arguing, Fulton tried
the skill of the *Nautilus* against the blockading ships of
the British Navy. Twice under cover of darkness, the
Nautilus approached the British brigs but her submerged progress was so slow that the enemy had sailed
off before she got within striking distance. At last
Napoleon decided not to support Fulton's invention.
The *Nautilus* was by this time over a year old, the salt
water had begun to corrode the metal and she had become very leaky. Fulton had failed and finally he broke
her up and sold her for scrap.

After trying, unsuccessfully, to sell his designs elsewhere Fulton went on to design the first paddle steamer
which finally made his fortune.

David

Sixty years later, during the American Civil War, the
idea of an underwater boat was revived yet again. The
Unionist forces from the North were having things all
their own way, especially at sea. Their Southern,
Confederate, opponents were running short of money to
buy arms. To earn more cash they had to ship out the
vast supplies of cotton that lay waiting at the dock-
side.

The Unionist ships lay in wait around every port,

attacking any cotton ship that attempted to leave and preventing arms supplies from entering. If the Confederates were to survive they had to smash the blockade. Any possible plan to do this was given very close attention.

In 1864 an inventor named Theodore Stoney got hold of an old gunboat, cut it down almost to the waterline and gave it an iron-plated roof. It was powered by a tiny steam engine attached to a two-bladed propeller and, because steam has to have an outlet pipe, it was unable to submerge completely. He named it *David* (after the David that slew Goliath). It was armed with 60 lbs of explosive which it carried on the end of a stout pole. This weapon was called a spar torpedo.

The *David*, looking a very unlikely vessel, set off to attack USS *New Ironsides*, a powerful Union ship lying off Charleston. Not surprisingly she was spotted by one of the sailors aboard the *Ironsides* who immediately fired on her.

The lieutenant in charge of the *David* just had time to ram the *Ironsides* with his torpedo, seriously damaging the ship. The blast also damaged the *David*, and her lieutenant decided to surrender, but to his amazement he was unable to do so. The terrified crew of the *Ironsides* were busily jumping overboard! So, after managing to rescue some of his own drowning crew, the lieutenant of the *David* limped off back to base.

The Unionists were badly shaken; although the *New Ironsides* was still afloat the sudden attack had them worried. When would this strange torpedo boat strike again, and where? Their men-of-war were kept ready for departure day and night and the deck watches were doubled.

The Confederates did, in fact, build more *David*-type boats but, due to the alert Unionist crews, who spotted the steam funnels sticking out of the water, they did not manage any more sneak attacks. Something better was needed.

The Confederates hoped it had arrived with the completion of yet another submarine-type vessel, the *Hunley*.

Hunley

The *Hunley* had been built by a Captain H. L. Hunley, an impractical man with a vivid imagination. He had started with a 25-foot metal boiler on which he had fitted two cone-shaped ends. Inside these end compartments he constructed ballast tanks that could be filled and emptied by hand. As in the days of the early submarines, she was driven by cranking a propeller, but this time it needed eight men, sitting side by side, to turn the crank!

She was steered by a wheel linked to a rudder at the stern. The captain had to guide her, submerge her and also control her guns. It was no easy task to crew the *Hunley* either; the boiler was so small that the men were unable to pass each other or even change positions.

The *Hunley*'s trials were a series of disasters. At her first attempt she dived nose down into the mud and refused to surface. All her crew were lost. She was raised and pumped dry but was then flooded by passing ships. This left only three survivors from two crews. Suddenly it became more difficult to get volunteers but Hunley refused to give up and recruited a third crew of which he took command. After a thorough examination of the boat and some special training of the crew he cast

off. This time the anchor chain became tangled with that
of another ship. Out of control, she hit the bottom and
all lives, including Hunley's, were lost.

The *Hunley* was now considered cursed and orders
were given for her to be broken up. Lieutenant George
Dixon was put in charge of the task but he decided to
give her one more trial, as the Confederates were still
desperate to break the blockade. His commanding
officer finally allowed him to go ahead and Dixon, with a
crew thought to be bent on suicide, set out.

It was the evening of February 17th, 1864. They intended to attack the *Housatonic*, a brand new sloop
which happened, unwisely as it turned out, to be anchored only two and a half miles away.

It was a perfect night, calm and cool, with enough
light mist on the surface of the water to disguise any sign
of the *Hunley*. At the very last minute she was spotted
but by then she was too near to come into the sights of
the sloop's big guns. In any case it was too late, the
torpedo had been well rammed into the hull of the *Housatonic*.

With one mighty blast the large ship was ripped apart
and it sank in just four minutes. The submarine, as an
underwater weapon, had, at long last, made its first killing.

There was no time for celebration, however, because
the *Hunley*'s gallant crew, in a ship that had been
doomed from the start, were dragged to the bottom
alongside the *Housatonic*. The *Hunley* had not been
able to get far enough away before the explosion.

The great problem with these early submarines had
now become clear to everybody. Driven merely by hand
they would never be fast or powerful enough to get

themselves out of trouble or deep enough in the water to be invisible from the enemy. They needed some sort of powerful machinery that could work underwater.

Plongeur

The French thought they had the answer in 1863 when they launched the first mechanically propelled submarine. The French Government took a serious interest in this new design and for sheer size the *Plongeur* was in a different class from any previous submarines.

Ships are usually measured by the amount of water they displace or move aside when floating normally. If the water that Fulton's *Nautilus* displaced could have been measured it would have weighed 9 tons. This new French submarine the *Plongeur* displaced 410 tons. She measured 140 feet long and 20 feet wide.

Her amazing size was due to the fact that she was driven by an engine that was run on compressed air. Most of the space was occupied by twenty-three large air tanks each 20 feet long and 4 feet across.

The safety of the crew had been thought about carefully and a watertight lifeboat had been provided which could be entered from inside the ship and released from a hatch on top. The explosives were attached to a long pole which was fixed to the bow. She looked like a gigantic swordfish; her appearance, at least, was frightening.

In 1865 she put to sea and *Plongeur* turned out to be a very good name for her. When she was not plunging to the bottom of the sea she was shooting up to the surface again. Her captain had to wrestle with the controls in a small space lit only by oil lamps, and her uncontrollable behaviour and unmanageable size were too much for him. After several trials it was decided that she took so much time and effort to sail that the crew would never have time to launch an attack!

Her other great defect, as with the earlier submarines, was her use of the spar torpedo. Being fixed on to the submarine it put the crew in almost as much danger as the ship it was attacking. So for the second time the French gave up the submarine boat.

The Great Submarine Race

The *Plongeur*, in spite of its lack of success, stirred the interest of inventors all over the world, and in the 1880s there are records of forty-two different attempts to construct an underwater boat. Submerging and surfacing were not a major difficulty – as early as 1800 Robert Fulton had used ballast tanks, filling them to submerge and emptying them to surface again. Hunley and other early inventors had used diving planes or fins. Both these ideas worked well and indeed are basic parts of the submarines we have today. The great problem was still the means of propelling the submarine both on and underneath the surface of the water.

In America, Sweden, Spain, Italy and France inventors were having moderate successes. Even in Britain there were inventors trying to draw their plans to the attention of a doubting Admiralty. In 1886 Campbell and Ash built the first large electrically powered submarine. During trials it became stuck in the bottom of the London Docks for some time. This did nothing to make Naval officials look more kindly on the idea of a submarine.

The newspapers reporting the story made the whole thing seem ridiculous and no more was ever heard of it. This was a pity as in spite of its faults it seemed to be better than anything being produced in any other country. After this British inventors became discouraged. There seemed to be little chance of selling submarines to the British Navy, which had the largest and most powerful fleet in the world and was quite sure that she did not need submarines to protect her. She was to find out, to her cost, that the submarine could be a dangerous weapon in the hands of the enemy.

John Holland, an Irishman who had emigrated to the USA, had been experimenting for twenty-five years with submarines. During this period he had launched five submarines, each one an improvement on the last. His new idea was to use two different motors:

1) an air-breathing petrol engine to run on the surface (similar to the engine used in a motor-car);
2) a non-breathing engine that used electric storage batteries for travelling underwater when air was very valuable.

To dive, Holland used Fulton's ballast tanks to pull the submarine beneath the surface of the water. He then used his electric motor to drive the submarine down. At the same time the diving planes (shown in the diagrams overleaf by the small white markings at either end of the hull), were set as in Figure 1.

The engine was then turned to the fastest possible speed. Once down to the right depth the diving planes were set to level off as in Figure 2.

To get to the surface again compressed air was blown into the ballast tanks to make the craft lighter. Figure 3

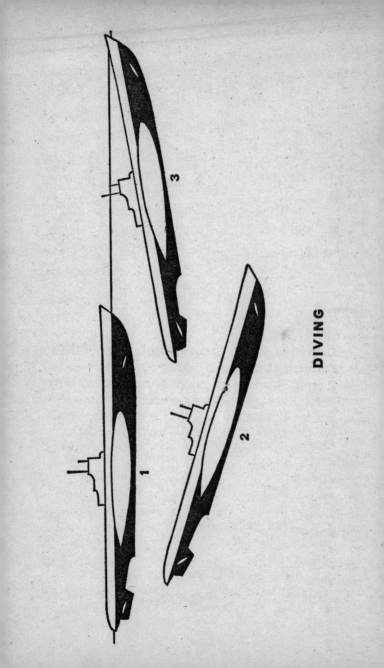

DIVING

shows diving planes set for a normal surfacing. This had to be done very slowly or she would have popped up to the surface like a cork.

For many years Holland had tried to interest the United States Navy in his boat but they felt that developing a strong fleet of surface boats was much more important. In 1888, just when Holland was about to give up, the American Navy suddenly announced a submarine design competition with a prize of $150,000 for the most practical design.

Holland won the competition and the prize money, but with a change of government in 1889 the idea of a submarine was yet again scrapped. Interest was revived in 1895 when another competition was held. After winning it a second time it still took five years of setbacks before Holland got permission to build the US Navy's first official submarine.

This was to be the most up to date of Holland's designs. She was powered on the surface by a 120-horsepower petrol engine, and underwater by a 150-horsepower electric motor run by storage batteries. The *Holland* measured only 58 feet long and 10 feet across and she could only submerge 60 feet. Surprisingly she had the same basic ideas as are used in today's most up to date atomic submarines.

One of the unsuccessful competitors, Simon Lake, invented a device that has become a standard item on submarines, the periscope – a long tube with an angled mirror at each end which makes it possible for someone in a submarine submerged a few feet beneath the surface to see what is happening above. It can turn in all directions and can also be pulled down inside.

By 1903 the US Navy was so excited by the *Holland*

that they gave her inventor instructions to have another six built. These became the world's first submarine fleet.

Other countries had been watching the submarine's progress carefully and it was not long before the British, realizing their mistake in taking the submarine so lightly, also invited Holland to design submarines for them. In 1901 the British Government ordered five.

In the meantime, the French slipped up by turning down a very advanced design from one of their own countrymen, a man called d'Equevilley. He then offered his design to the German Navy, who snapped it up. It was to become the famous U (Unterseeboot) 1, great-grandfather of the dreaded U-boats which were to destroy hundreds of ships in both world wars, some of which were French.

The Whitehead Torpedo

At the same time other inventors were experimenting with torpedoes that could actually move through the water alone. The most successful of these was built by a British engineer, Robert Whitehead. In 1870 he sold his torpedo designs to the British Government for £150,000. Looking like 14-foot long bullets they carried 67 lbs of explosives in their noses and were housed in the bows of the submarine to be fired like a gun when submerged.

The Diesel Engine

From 1909 onwards the navies of the world began to fit their submarines with a new type of engine that was powered by oil instead of petrol, thus making them cheaper and less dangerous to run. As this engine, originally invented by a German, Rudolf Diesel, burned only half as much fuel as the petrol engine it also meant that the submarines could prowl the high seas for much longer periods without refuelling.

The Submarine at War

At the outbreak of World War I in August 1914, Britain had almost total command of the sea. For this reason alone Germany looked very closely into the possibilities of the submarine boat as a weapon and by the time war broke out, she had built twenty U-boats. At the same time Britain had seventy-four submarines but many of them were out of date and used mainly for training.

On the first two days of war the German U-boats put to sea before dawn and formed a line of outposts to defend their country. When the expected British Fleet did not appear, instructions were given for ten of the submarines to go out and look for the enemy. Although they did not manage to attack any ships their periscopes were seen by British warships and the cruiser *Birmingham* rammed the U-15 and broke her clean in half.

The sighting of these U-boats frightened the proud British Fleet, especially as there was no way of detecting them in 1914 except by their periscopes. U-boat patrols continued to be sent out and finally the U-21, charging her batteries on the surface off the Scottish coast, sighted a patrolling cruiser *Pathfinder*. In spite of bad weather and heaving seas, the U-21 torpedoed her and within four minutes she had disappeared beneath the waves. The sea-wolf had tasted blood for the first time.

This was only a warning. On September 20th the U-9, an out-of-date submarine hampered by a faulty compass and an exhausted crew, came upon three armoured British cruisers. Somehow she managed to torpedo and sink all of them. So twenty-six men in a 450-ton submarine had been responsible for the lives of 1,400 men and had destroyed 36,000 tons of enemy warships. The submarine had finally grown up to be a powerful and effective weapon!

During the First and the Second World Wars submarines went from strength to strength, terrorizing vessels that sailed on the surface of the sea. The U-boats almost brought victory to Germany in both wars and it was only the success of anti-submarine devices like mines, depth-charges and radar that helped Britain and her allies to keep the sea-wolves at bay.

The Nuclear Submarine

Little change took place in the basic design of the submarine after the invention of the diesel engine at the turn of the century. Naval engineers worked hard to improve the reliability and safety of the submarine but were still hampered by the electric storage batteries which, when wet, gave off poisonous chlorine gas fumes and sometimes blew up. The arrival of the nuclear-powered submarine after the Second World War changed all this. After nine years of experiment the first ship to be driven by nuclear power began her trials in Connecticut in January 1955.

Her whole shape was different, with a bulbous rounded bow like a large silent whale – silent, of course, because there were no longer exhaust fumes bubbling out of her tubes. Her air-purifying system made it possible for her to stay under for weeks at a time. In fact she was the first true submarine in that she was actually built to do all her travelling underwater.

In the following years many more nuclear submarines were built and now they are manoeuvring, diving and criss-crossing seas that were impossibly remote in the days before nuclear power. 1960 was a remarkable year for the submarine. In May an American submarine, *Triton*, with twin nuclear reactors completed the first non-stop underwater voyage round the earth. In July the USS *George Washington* fired the first Polaris nuclear missile from beneath the sea, which hit its target a thousand miles away. In October the first British nuclear submarine, HMS *Dreadnought*, was launched on Trafalgar Day.

Britain now has nine nuclear-powered submarines, four of which are equipped with Polaris missiles. These are the *Resolution*, *Renown*, *Repulse* and *Revenge*. The great military advantage of nuclear submarines as carriers of rocket-type weapons is that they can launch an attack underwater from practically anywhere in the world. This constant threat from submarines armed with nuclear weapons helps to keep peace between the major powers; no one dares to provoke the enemy into using such a lethal weapon.

Chapter 2

The Phantom of the Marmara

The First World War marks the first time in history when both sides were able to attack each other with submarines that actually worked. Although they had grown in size and were now 800-ton giants compared with the 100-ton *Holland*, submarines in 1914 were still slow, unreliable weapons. It took a brave sailor to serve on one.

At the outbreak of the war, submarines were built to spend most of their time on the surface where they could move fairly quickly but were an easy target for more heavily-armed surface ships. When they did submerge they could only go down about 100 feet and their highest speed under water was around eight knots. While under the water the crew had to work with a sickening smell of diesel fumes and little oxygen in the air. The conditions were so unpleasant that the submarines usually tried to surface again as soon as possible. To live in a submarine for weeks on end was an extremely uncomfortable, not to mention dangerous, way of defending one's country.

However, the submarine still had the attractive advantage of becoming 'invisible' when required and once she was safely under the water her enemies had no means of attacking her.

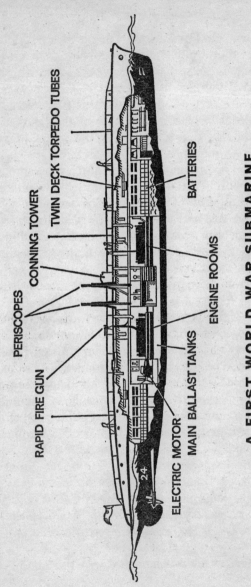

A FIRST WORLD WAR SUBMARINE

RAPID FIRE GUN

PERISCOPES

CONNING TOWER

TWIN DECK TORPEDO TUBES

BATTERIES

ENGINE ROOMS

MAIN BALLAST TANKS

ELECTRIC MOTOR

This new kind of warfare brought with it a different breed of sailor, commanded by cool-headed, courageous captains who seemed to thrive on the discomfort and unexpected dangers to be found in these new underwater weapons. One such leader was Lieutenant-Commander Martin Nasmith, captain of the famous E-11 submarine. His daring exploits in the Sea of Marmara will long be remembered in British naval history.

The Sea of Marmara was one of the most important seas in World War I. It ran through the middle of Turkey, an ally of Germany in her fight against Britain, France and Russia. It extended inside Turkey like a large pocket and it was obvious that any ships that managed to enter it would be in a strong position to attack the Turks.

A narrow passage of water called the Dardanelles separated the Aegean Sea from the Marmara. As this was the British Allies' most likely route into the Marmara and the Turkish capital Constantinople, it was more heavily guarded than any other stretch of water in the world. The banks of the Dardanelles were packed with torpedo tubes and guns of all shapes and sizes. There were thirteen rows of minefields, an unlucky number for any passing vessel, and glaring searchlights to give permanent day-light. The Turks were prepared for trouble!

It arrived on March 18th, 1915, in the shape of eighteen majestic battleships with huge grumbling guns. They penetrated the Dardanelles but after only a few miles three were sunk, three badly damaged and 700 men were dead. The Fleet soon retreated. They did not return.

The next attack was launched by British and French

troops who landed on the Gallipoli peninsula and tried to knock out the Turkish defences from behind. The attack was to last eight long months. For the British to beat the Turkish armies on land, it was important to cut off the Turkish supply lines, the ships which brought troops, food and ammunition from Constantinople and Panderma to Gallipoli. As Allied ships could not get through the Dardanelles, and aircraft bombers were not properly developed, the only possible hope was to use the newest weapon, the submarine.

Five Allied submarines had entered the Marmara before the E-11. Four of them soon came to grief but one, the E-14, spent three weeks inside Turkey, attacking enemy ships, and her greatest success was the sinking of a large troop transporter *Guy Djemal*. This threw the Turks into a panic. The idea of the new submarines frightened most people but to think of unknown numbers running riot in the middle of their country thoroughly alarmed them. They had no idea there was only one!

Martin Nasmith was very impressed with the E-14's exploits and the panic she had caused, and hoped his submarine, the E-11, would be chosen for a similar mission. His greatest ambition was to be the first enemy ship to enter the harbour of Constantinople. No enemy ship had managed to enter for 500 years but Nasmith was an optimistic man!

Unfortunately, the E-11 developed serious engine trouble and while he waited for it to be mended, Nasmith found out as much as he could about the Dardanelles, its currents, the positioning and types of its many guns and how to deal with these hazards when he found them. Finally, the work on the E-11 was finished

and on May 19th, 1915, she set out on her first mission
into the Sea of Marmara. She was a large, well-built
boat containing ten torpedoes to use in her five tubes. As
it was to be a long mission she carried lots of extra
equipment and the conditions inside were very cramped. Her three officers and twenty-eight men were even
denied the luxury of hammocks in this boat; they had to
sleep in any nook or cranny that they could find on or
under the machinery.

The journey through the minefields was easier than
they had expected, although there were several heart-
stopping moments when they heard the grating of the
mines' mooring cables scraping along the E-11's hull.
Nasmith put his periscope up once for a look around
and, caught in the glare of a searchlight, was shot at and
almost rammed by a destroyer.

Throwing on her cloak of invisibility the E-11 had no
trouble in slipping away and at 1.30 PM on the 20th she
arrived safe in the Sea of Marmara. The air in the submarine was very stale by this time; in fact, the oxygen
level was so low that even matches would not burn. The
crew, suffering from the after-effects of their adventure
and the enclosed conditions on the boat, were forced to
wait until dark before daring to bring the E-11 to the
surface. It was a great relief to breathe the welcome
fresh air again, even if they were deep in enemy ter-
ritory.

On the following day the E-11 crept around the Sea of
Marmara looking for the enemy ships that were bringing troops and supplies up to the front line in Gallipoli.
They were amazed to find the Sea quite empty! Obviously, word had got around quickly that another 'submarine', a word that struck terror into Turkish hearts,

was on the rampage in the Marmara. On the morning of the 22nd, their luck changed when they caught sight of an empty troop carrier some way ahead. Whilst chasing it they were in turn set upon by a Turkish gunboat. Nasmith sent the first of his torpedoes into her but whilst sinking she returned a 6-lb shell that made a hole through the top of the E-11's periscope. A perfect shot!

After tearing off the broken periscope top and plugging up the hole they continued on their way. Their next success was the cargo ship *Nagara*. Before they sank her the crew set off in lifeboats and, after overpowering *Nagara*'s crew, helped themselves to the fresh food they found on board. Since their own fresh food had run out the crew had been living on corned beef and ship's biscuits, so butter and eggs made a very welcome change! After a good supper Nasmith allowed shifts of men to go bathing in the warm sea water. After days in the submarine's clammy interior this must have been a great treat.

Impatient at being unable to find any enemy battleships to attack, Nasmith decided next to try his hand at the capital Constantinople. He knew that many prize ships were anchored there not daring to brave the Marmara whilst enemy submarines were lurking. He also knew that there were strong currents around the harbour which would make the trip dangerous, but his ambition got the better of him.

Despite the currents the submerged E-11 passed through the harbour entrance on May 25th and into Constantinople. After the empty sea behind him Nasmith now saw a completely different picture through his periscope. The harbour was packed with vessels of every kind. The difficulty was choosing what to shoot first! Finally, he picked out a large troop carrier which was anchored very close to another ship. With luck he might get both of them with one shot!

Taking very careful aim he fired his first torpedo but immediately it left the boat it slewed around in the wrong direction, jumped wildly in the air and then disappeared from view. Not daring to waste a moment Nasmith fired another torpedo and this time it homed straight on to the target. Before he had time to congratulate himself Nasmith was horrified to see that his first faulty torpedo was now heading back towards the E-11, having made a complete circle of the harbour!

There was only just time to get the little submarine under before the runaway torpedo swished overhead and finally exploded against one of the harbour wharves. It was a close shave and after sinking only one ship, *Stamboul*, the E-11 made a hasty get-away. The currents pulled at her much harder this time. Suddenly it seemed as if she was in the middle of a whirlpool and spinning like a top, but she pulled herself loose and soon she was on her way back into the Marmara. The crew, as one man, breathed a sigh of relief.

Behind her in Constantinople there was pandemonium. Convinced that Allied forces had landed, many of the Turks fled from the city. Shops were closed up and waiting troops were sent back to their barracks. There would be no more ships leaving Constantinople that day! Pleased with his crew, Nasmith decided to make the following day a holiday, allowing them plenty of time to sleep and swim in the Marmara. At the same time he made sure the torpedoes were carefully overhauled; he did not want any more accidents!

After the day of rest the crew of the E-11 stalked the

Sea of Marmara once more. She was chased twice on the 27th, once by a destroyer bent on ramming her, and once by a small yacht which suddenly uncovered a deck gun and proceeded to fire at her.

The next day began more promisingly when they managed to board a supply ship and blow her up with explosives. Soon afterwards a transport ship was sighted and Nasmith sent off a torpedo from the starboard beam, but this one turned out to be another dud. It hit the ship but did not explode. After the ship had left the scene the crew went off in search of the torpedo. They found it a couple of miles away floating innocently on the surface of the sea. Nasmith, without stopping to think of the danger involved, pulled off his clothes and, taking only a spanner with him, jumped over the side!

With extreme care he removed the explosive from the torpedo's nose and swam back to the boat with it. The crew then hoisted up the 17-foot long bullet in a giant sling and lowered it back into the boat through the forward hatch. As torpedoes were very precious, and could not be replaced, Nasmith was determined to get his full value out of them by using them more than once.

The E-11 spent another week searching the Marmara but the Turks were taking no chances with their important ships. Nasmith could find nothing on which to spend his last torpedoes, so on June 6th they decided to return home. Apart from the new set of torpedoes they needed, Nasmith felt that a gun mounted on the deck would be extremely useful on a mission of this kind. He was determined to have one fitted when they got back to Malta. *If* they got back . . . there were still the treacherous Dardanelles waiting for them.

The sun was just coming up on the 7th when the E-11

submerged at the Dardanelles approach for the long run home. She had one torpedo left in her tubes which Nasmith had been saving in the hope of meeting a battle-ship on the way through. Several times on their patrol they had glimpsed the mighty Turkish battleship *Barbarossa* and they had high hopes that she would be patrolling the Dardanelles, a sitting target for their last torpedo. There was no sign of the *Barbarossa* so instead Nasmith fired his last torpedo at an empty transport ship and sank her. This made a total for the mission of seven ships and one gunboat.

As they passed under the second minefield the E-11 suddenly began to jerk up and down in the water almost as if she was being plucked at by an unseen hand. Nasmith was disturbed; was it the current playing tricks on them, or was the E-11 developing a serious fault? Acting quickly he gave orders for the submarine to rise to 20 feet below the surface. He raised his periscope in the hope of finding a clue to the E-11's odd behaviour and was horrified to see a large horned ball sitting on the deck of the E-11. A mine! Somehow the mine's cable had become caught between the submarine and her port diving plane. As he did not dare to try to clear it under the noses of the big guns up above Nasmith had no choice but to take it along with them. Nasmith decided to keep the secret to himself. It seemed unlikely that the E-11 could finish its journey in one piece while carrying such a deadly passenger, but telling the crew about it wasn't going to help.

Nasmith crossed his fingers and gave orders to dive. He then climbed inside the conning tower and watched the mine through a porthole as it was pulled down into the depths with them. There was nothing he could do apart from trying to keep the little submarine as straight and steady as possible. The worst moment would come when they had to dive much deeper under the third minefield. The dive was very smooth and apart from the usual rasp of mine cables against the E-11's hull, everything went well. Every moment Nasmith expected the E-11's own mine to hit another one and cause a double explosion!

After what seemed like hours one of his officers informed him that they were through the minefield. By now there was a very happy atmosphere on board the E-11. As far as the crew were concerned they were home and dry. Nasmith alone dreaded giving the order to surface as he knew it meant moving the hydroplane which would shift the mine's cable and bring it nearer to the conning tower! The little submarine slowly nosed its way up until it was just below the surface. The mine, amazingly, was bobbing along just in front of them. By this time, of course, it had been noticed by some of the crew.

They had now reached the safety of home waters and they could hear the propellers of a destroyer coming towards them. Knowing it was friendly, Nasmith sent a man into the conning tower to be ready to hoist their flag just in case the destroyer attempted to ram them. The time had now come for the E-11 to shake off her unwelcome guest. Nasmith gave orders for the submarine to go quickly into reverse. As she did so the rush of water in the opposite direction pushed the mine's cable off the hydroplane and, weighed down by its heavy sinker, it fell harmlessly to the bottom of the bay.

Delighted at seeing the last of their deadly cargo the

crew brought the E-11 to the surface and hoisted her flag. She was met by resounding cheers from the men on the destroyer who had been sent to look for her. The reports of her amazing 20-day patrol had been passed on to the men and Nasmith and his crew were already considered heroes. Afterwards Nasmith was awarded the Victoria Cross for gallantry on patrol.

Whilst the E-11 was being overhauled in Malta and fitted with a 12-lb gun, the worried Turks were also busy. Determined to keep out the submarine menace they fixed a steel net like a gigantic spider's web across the narrowest part of the Dardanelles. Satisfied with their work, they sat back and waited for the flies.

The first two were E-12 and E-7. Both submarines found the nets troublesome but far from impossible. They approached them at full speed and rammed them repeatedly until by sheer brute force they snapped the $2\frac{1}{2}$-inch thick wires, making a hole large enough to squeeze through. When E-7 returned after a 24-day patrol Nasmith was sent once more into the Marmara. The Turks were now sending more and more of their supplies on fleets of small sailing boats called dhows and it became necessary for two submarines to patrol the sea at the same time.

E-11's second trip up the Dardanelles was more hazardous than her first. The mines had been placed lower in the water and two or three times the crew felt them actually knocking on the hull. Surprisingly, there were no explosions. If the E-11 had nine lives she could not now have many left. Nasmith hoped to avoid the new net altogether by diving underneath it but even at 110 feet the submarine was brought to an abrupt halt. He then tried the ramming method used by the two submarines before him and E-11 soon broke her way through. After leaving the net behind, Nasmith soon had his periscope up again looking for targets and, with one carefully placed torpedo, sank an empty transport ship lying at anchor. He now felt he was back in the battle again and doing something to help the British troops who were fighting for their lives in the peninsula.

On the afternoon of the following day the E-11 met up with the E-14 in the middle of the Marmara, deep in the heart of enemy country. It must have been an extraordinary sight to see the two captains of these strange new machines standing in their conning towers shouting to each other across the waves.

Two days later the E-11 found what she had been looking for since her very first day in the Marmara.

A wisp of black smoke on the horizon sighted through Nasmith's binoculars betrayed the passing of the only Turkish battleship left, the elusive *Barbarossa*! As she was sailing towards them Nasmith could do nothing but watch as the mighty warship grew larger and larger inside his tiny periscope. She was a terrifying sight and confronting her the submarine captain felt his courage begin to desert him.

He still had a long mission ahead of him and he dared not risk using more than one torpedo on the *Barbarossa*. He desperately hoped that his aim would be true and that the torpedo would not be another faulty one. His precious bullet hit the ship's large ammunition store and there was a mighty explosion which tilted the big ship towards her starboard side. She immediately changed course and made for the beach in the hope of sinking in shallower water; but it was too late. There was another

large explosion and she rolled over and disappeared
from view.

Later that day Nasmith had a signal for help from
Boyle of the E-14 who was shooting at an empty troop
carrier. The E-11 rushed over to help her and had his
first bit of bad luck. The deck gun, of which he was so
proud, exploded whilst firing, sending the poor gunner
flying through the air and into the sea. He was dragged
out only bruised but the gun mounting was almost split
apart. At first glance it seemed beyond repair but after
hours of patient labour the determined crew managed to
get it working again.

After sinking an important coal-carrying ship and
some abandoned trading dhows, Nasmith turned his attention to the Berlin-Baghdad railway which in places
ran close to the coast. He realized that although the two
submarines were cutting the Turkish sea routes, supplies were still getting through to Gallipoli by train. If
only something could be done to disrupt the rail routes
as well! The easiest place to attack the railway was
about thirty miles down the coast from Constantinople
where it crossed an ironwork viaduct. It was quite close
to the sea and well within the range of the E-11's gun.
As soon as she opened fire, however, the larger guns of
the Turkish shore patrols bombarded her and she was
forced to make a hasty underwater retreat!

Something less obvious and more cunning was
needed and D'Oyley Hughes, Nasmith's second-in-com-
mand, came up with a daring plan. D'Oyley Hughes, a
tough energetic Irishman, was dropped over the side of
the E-11 at 2 AM on the morning of August 21st. The
submarine had crept in as close as possible to the coast
and Hughes swam ashore pushing in front of him a raft

carrying enough explosives to blow up the viaduct.

Hughes landed the raft safely and put on his dry uniform (if he were caught out of uniform he could be shot as a spy) and taking a pistol, a bayonet, a whistle and the explosives he set out for the viaduct. It took him half an hour to find it in the dark and he was disappointed to find it under heavy guard. Whilst circling around it looking for a possible opening, Hughes jumped over a low wall and landed in the middle of a hen run. The squawking and cackling of the bad tempered birds was enough to waken the dead, but he quickly made for the opposite wall and was over it before anyone came to see what the noise was about. After this he abandoned his first plan and decided to blow up the track itself.

Unfortunately, he had to fire his pistol to light the fuse of the explosive charge and this alerted the Turkish guards who chased him back towards the shore. With rifle bullets whistling round his ears Hughes scrambled down the cliffs towards the beach. He had almost reached it when he heard a terrific explosion. Knowing that the railway must now be out of action for some time, he swam out to sea looking for the E-11, blowing his whistle loudly at the same time. There was no sign of the E-11, and he realized that his flight from the enemy had taken him farther down the coast than he thought. Tired and worried, he swam back to the shore and trudged back up the coast. It was daylight before Hughes found the E-11, which was under fire from the Turks. Once more he swam out and this time was hauled on board by his delighted comrades.

The E-11 spent another thirteen days in the Marmara before returning home to another heartwarming reception. She made only one other sortie into the Marmara, returning in December after a record-breaking patrol of forty-seven days. The fight for the Gallipoli peninsula was now over. After eight months of fighting and many deaths on both sides, the remaining Allied troops were forced to leave Gallipoli and the Turks had their country to themselves once more. It had been a useless battle wasting many lives, but war is often like this.

The submarine emerged with a new reputation. It had shown an unbelieving world how good commanders and crews could use this new weapon to excellent advantage. In the Dardanelles campaign it had succeeded when all else had failed.

Chapter 3

Rescue by Diving Bell

On May 3rd, 1939, a new submarine was launched. Her British and American designers now had twenty-five years of experience to draw on, both in peacetime and war, and the result was thought to be the last word in safe submarine design.

The *Squalus*, Latin for Shark, the latest addition to the US Navy's Fleet, was 310 feet long and displaced 1,456 tons. Her crew of fifty-six were skilled, hand-picked men, many of whom had spent long spells at sea in other submarines and were delighted to have been chosen for duty on this one.

After launching, all submarines have various care-fully worked out diving trials, from the simple un-hurried dives in calm water to emergency dives on the run whilst firing torpedoes. The *Squalus* completed seventeen such dives satisfactorily and the designers dis-covered only tiny flaws to put right.

The crew were pleased to find her faster and easier to manoeuvre than previous submarines they had served on, and also better equipped and roomier. It was nice to be able to lift a mug of tea to your mouth without put-ting your elbow in somebody's eye!

On May 23rd she sailed out from Portsmouth, New

Hampshire, to make her eighteenth dive. Her captain,
Lieutenant Oliver Naquin, had already detailed his crew
to their various stations in the compartments of the boat
and they were all prepared for diving.

The *Squalus* was divided into six separate sections:
there was a torpedo room at each end of the boat, two
engine rooms towards the stern and a control room in
the middle with rooms on both sides containing the batteries which charged the engines.

At 8.30 AM Lieutenant Naquin ordered full speed on
both engines and soon the steady ticking-over increased
to a roar as the *Squalus* reached the sixteen knots
necessary for this particular dive, which was a mock
'crash' dive whilst under attack.

Meanwhile, the commander was checking his control
board. This was a set of lights in the shape of a Christmas tree with each bulb representing one opening in
the hull of the ship, e.g. conning tower or torpedo
hatch covers. These obviously had to be firmly sealed
before a dive could take place. As each opening was
closed in rotation, the lights on the control board
winked from red to green until finally the board
was completely green. In this way the captain and his
officers could see at a glance when the whole ship was
watertight.

'Stand by to dive!' came the captain's order and immediately the ship was ringing with that spine-chilling
sound, the 'ooogh-aaagh' of the ship's klaxon. The
Squalus, now powered by her large batteries, slipped
swiftly into the ocean and was gone.

The crew visibly relaxed: everything had gone according to plan. This was going to be another successful
dive. Unexpectedly, there was the strident shrill of the

control room phone and a frantic voice shouted over the line.

'Sir! The engine rooms are flooding!'

Several pairs of eyes swivelled round to the Christmas tree. All the lights were green.

The impossible had happened: although the board reported everything to be sealed, somehow a large fresh-air valve in the engine rooms had for some completely unknown reason, after sealing satisfactorily, opened up again! It seemed as if the whole sea was pounding its way into the engine rooms.

Naquin recovered quickly and shouted: 'Blow out the main ballast tanks!' The cry, 'Take her up, take her up!' echoed through the ship.

Her crew, sensing the urgency, blew the main tanks immediately. For a moment the *Squalus* halted in her headlong dive and hesitated midway between the surface and the ocean floor, but the sea was still pouring into the engine rooms drowning her motors and adding several tons per second to her weight. It was a nightmare situation.

In any such emergency the crew are trained to carry out one very important instruction without needing to be told: the closing of the watertight doors so that water can get no farther.

The watertight doors between the after battery room and the control room were now most important, as electrician Lloyd Maness was quick to realize. Already water from the flooding engine rooms was rushing uphill through the battery room towards the control room. Normally the large watertight door would have been easy to close, but now, with the submarine slanting stern down, Maness had to lift it towards him like a very heavy trapdoor. Twice he paused to let seamen out as they struggled spluttering and coughing through the swiftly rising water.

When the water began to splash over his shoes Maness could afford to wait no longer. With a final desperate heave he pulled the door closed. It was this act alone that saved the lives of thirty-three men, for the time being at least.

It was 8.45 AM. Within five minutes of starting a successful dive the *Squalus*, with twenty-six of her men already dead, was lying crippled under 240 feet of water. She had no heating or lighting and the temperature outside her hull was only a degree above freezing point.

Amazingly, there was no panic. The submariners brought out flashlights and lanterns kept on board for such an emergency and soon an eerie glow lit the pale faces of the men in the control room. Naquin then tried to make telephone contact with the after torpedo room, the only other compartment that could have been sealed off against the torrent of water. When there was no reply he had to assume that there were no other survivors.

Naquin ordered the firing of a red smoke rocket, the submarine distress signal. The next move was to send up the marker buoy. This was a bright orange buoy shaped like an oil drum. It contained a telephone and was linked directly to the submarine by a cable. It bore the grim message 'SUBMARINE SUNK HERE – TELEPHONE INSIDE'.

Naquin's next task was not a pleasant one. He had to call a roll of the survivors. Of the crew of 56 sailors and 3 civilians only 33 were left. The survivors were severely

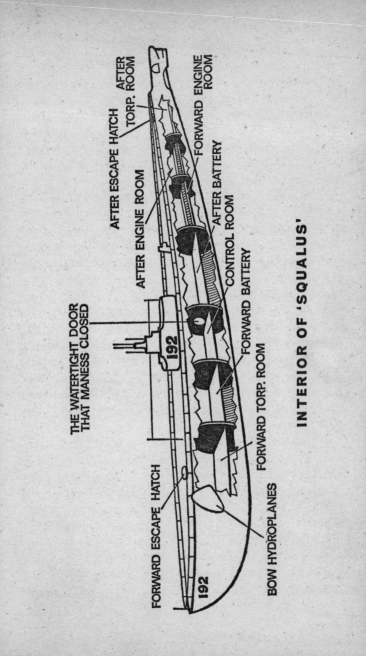

THE WATERTIGHT DOOR
THAT MANESS CLOSED

FORWARD ESCAPE HATCH

192

BOW HYDROPLANES

FORWARD TORP. ROOM

FORWARD BATTERY

CONTROL ROOM

AFTER BATTERY

AFTER ENGINE ROOM

AFTER ESCAPE HATCH   AFTER
                     TORP.
                     ROOM

FORWARD ENGINE
ROOM

192

INTERIOR OF 'SQUALUS'

shocked. Men they had been working with only minutes before were now sealed for ever behind the control room door. The captain pulled himself together for there was still a lot to do for those who remained alive.

He began by making a tour of inspection of the water-tight forward part of the boat. He divided the crew into two groups; one half went forward into the bow torpedo room and the other half stayed in the control room.

The batteries in the forward battery room were already splashed with water and, as the combination can give off the deadly chlorine gas, he decided to leave it empty. In any case the cold was now becoming so severe that it seemed better for the men to huddle close together with as many blankets and towels as they could find to wrap around themselves. He also ordered the men to lie quietly and only move if it was unavoidable. Every bit of oxygen in the air was vital for their survival. Resting and shallow breathing would use it up less quickly.

The *Squalus* was due to surface again at 9.40 AM and until then no one at the Portsmouth Navy Yard would miss them. Apart from sending up regular rocket flares all they could do now was to sit it out.

When 9.40 AM arrived without word from the *Squalus* nobody at Portsmouth was unduly worried. It was not uncommon for submarines to be a little late. After an hour, however, the duty officer in the Portsmouth radio room reported to his superiors that the *Squalus* was an hour late in reporting in.

The matter was now in the hands of Rear-Admiral Cyrus Cole who got on to the Coastguard station on the nearby Isle of Shoals. They reported no sign of *Squalus* and to Cole it now seemed possible that something might be seriously wrong. Alarmed, he rushed over to the *Squalus'* sister submarine, *Sculpin*, with the compass bearings of the *Squalus'* last dive. He told her captain Lieutenant-Commander Warren Wilkin to search at once for any sign of the *Squalus*.

Cole then set off to alert the nearest submarine rescue vessel the *Falcon*, a converted World War I minesweeper. It carried one of the five recent and, as yet, untried rescue inventions known as the Momsem-McCann diving bells. By an unlucky chance most of the crew of the *Falcon* were on leave as she was having her yearly overhaul and the McCann diving bell wasn't even on board. However, her captain promised to have the *Falcon* on her way just as quickly as possible.

Down in the *Squalus* the crew continued to send up their rockets at frequent intervals and soon after noon when there was no sign of help they made themselves lunch of tinned sardines, beans and evaporated milk.

At 12.40 PM another flare arched through the sky and this time its smoky trail was seen by one of *Sculpin*'s lookouts. Ten minutes later the *Squalus'* crew heard the sound of propellers approaching and excitedly sent up another flare. This one exploded 300 yards in front of the *Sculpin* and her lookouts then spotted the brave little orange marker bobbing on the waves.

The buoy was brought up on board and Captain Wilkin took only a moment to snatch out the telephone. There was just time for the officer at the other end to give brief details of the *Squalus'* plight before a sudden fierce wave pitched *Sculpin* high into the air and snapped the telephone cable.

Meanwhile, Admiral Cole, himself an ex-submariner and particularly concerned about the *Squalus*' fate, set off in the only seaworthy boat left in the harbour, an old tug called *Penacook*. It was slow and the engines coughed alarmingly but it got Cole to the scene in time to direct rescue operations. In New London, where the rescue ship *Falcon* was berthed, police and shore patrols were busily rounding up the crew members who were on leave and the few men left on duty were striving to get the boilers of the old ship going. Steam was necessary in order to lift the diving bell back on board and also, of course, to propel the engine.

Ten minutes after leaving, the news about the snapped telephone cable came through to Cole aboard the *Penacook*. This was really bad news. The telephone, apart from being a vital means of communication with the imprisoned men, also provided a cable which a diver could easily follow right down to the submarine. Without this cable it could take hours or even days to pinpoint exactly *Squalus*' position on the bottom.

At 3.15 Admiral Cole arrived at the anchored *Sculpin* where he changed ships. His main concern was to somehow contact the *Squalus* again. The crew of the *Sculpin* had dropped another marker buoy in the water where they imagined the first buoy to have been but with the changing currents this obviously could not be taken as a reliable guide. Cole ordered buoys to be released 100 yards north and south of the probable position of the *Squalus* and to start dragging the sea bottom between the two points.

Inside the *Squalus*, now suddenly out of touch again, the waiting was awful. Time dragged by painfully slowly and the extreme cold in the ship became almost unbearable. Most of the men's clothing and blankets were now sodden from the water lapping on the floor of the boat and their breathing was becoming laboured. Nobody tried to speak because the effort was too great. To help things a little they sprinkled a tin of a special powder on the deck floor, which absorbed some of the poisonous carbon dioxide that the men were breathing out.

Each man had a Momsem lung to use in case the lack of air eventually began to cause suffocation. This lung was a very simple version of our present-day aqua lung. It took the shape of a sealed rubber carrier bag which was hung around the neck and fastened by straps around the waist.

'Swede' Momsem was a seasoned submariner who had worked hard on these safety devices, testing everything personally many times. The men in the *Squalus* considered him quite a hero and it was agreed that if they were to escape, Momsem's lungs and diving bells would probably play an important part.

When the crew heard the propellers of the *Penacook* arriving, their spirits lifted; friends were at hand. At last something was going to be done. But as the tug began to zig-zag overhead, it slowly became clear that their actual position was still a mystery to their would-be rescuers.

However, unknown to them, more help was now on the way. A cruiser with medical facilities, the *Brooklyn*, was already steaming towards the scene from New York. She also had on board thousands of feet of air hose that might be needed for pumping water from the *Squalus*. Close behind followed the tug *Sagamore* with salvage equipment necessary for lifting the *Squalus* from the bottom.

Boats of various kinds and from various directions were making for the wounded ship and the most promising of these was *Falcon*. Complete with diving bell and divers she had somehow managed to set off from her New London berth only an hour after hearing that the *Squalus* was definitely 'down'. A remarkable exercise in cool-headed efficiency!

At 5.25 PM the tug *Wandank* arrived to help *Penacook* in her frustrating task of dragging the sea bed. They used umbrella-shaped grappling hooks in an attempt to catch the deck rail of the *Squalus*. Their job was made doubly difficult by the number of rotting old hulks that were also lying on the bottom. At 7.30 PM they finally snagged the right wreck; this time it was the *Squalus*.

When the *Wandank* arrived she began to call *Squalus* on her powerful radio and *Squalus* received the signals very clearly. The rescuers wanted as much information as possible about the submarine's position and present condition. Naquin racked his brains for some way to reply. Stripping the conning tower of its warm cork insulation he organized relays of signalmen to hammer on the hull of the ship with metal mallets.

This was exhausting for the men and as the *Wandank* kept repeating her questions it seemed as if the sound was not carrying to the surface. Naquin encouraged them to carry on, however, mainly to keep the men's spirits up. Any kind of action was better than just sitting and waiting. At 9.30 PM the news came through to the *Squalus*, 'Believe we have grapnel attached to your ship'.

Everything that could be done for the *Squalus* had now been completed and only the arrival of *Falcon* and her diving bell could set a rescue bid in motion. The sailors of the ships gathered helplessly above *Squalus* could only sit and wait and ask themselves: 'How much longer will she be? Even if she does get here in time, will this new contraption work?' The only person with even the remotest idea was Lieutenant George Sharpe, the *Falcon*'s captain, and he was still 150 miles away and *Falcon* was at that moment running into thick fog!

Whilst Lieutenant Sharpe was having to go the long way round to avoid the fog and the *Penacook* was grappling for the *Squalus*, 'Swede' Momsem, one of the inventors of the rescue bell, was splashing down in a seaplane near Portsmouth with two doctors and a diving expert. They were immediately rushed on to a Coast-guard cutter for the trip out to the *Sculpin*.

It was not until 4.15 AM the next day that Commander McCann, the other half of the team of inventors, arrived with another twelve divers. They had also run into the bad weather. There was still no sign of *Falcon*.

Admiral Cole had by this time put 'Swede' Momsem in charge of all diving operations and a message to this effect was sent down to the *Squalus*. In spite of their very weak condition the news cheered the crew enormously. Momsem himself had risked his life so many times in the same sort of conditions just to perfect his machine, that they put all their trust in him now.

At 5.25 the old minesweeper *Falcon* finally rushed up bringing the bad weather with her. The complicated business of mooring directly above the *Squalus* began. It was a difficult mooring as the high winds and wild sea kept pulling her in the wrong direction. It was important to get it perfect as the diver's life and also the lives of those in the submarine depended on it. It took four hours of pitching and rolling before *Falcon* was finally secured by four anchors.

The diver Martin Sibitsky, dressed in his heavy metal boots, cumbersome suit and large round helmet was finally lowered over the side and down the *Penacook*'s line. It was 10.14 AM. Sibitsky was breathing a mixture of oxygen and helium which was pumped through to him from the ship and he had to take great care that this long breathing tube did not get squashed or snagged. It was his lifeline so his descent had to be very slow.

The water grew gradually darker as he went deeper but suddenly the giant bulk of the *Squalus* began to take shape. His heavy boots were soon clumping on the hull of the submarine and he was delighted to find that the *Penacook* had luckily snagged the hand rail of the *Squalus* only a few feet away from the escape hatch he was aiming for.

He reported back to Momsem and the down-haul cable for the rescue chamber was lowered to him. Twice Sibitsky tried to grab it and failed but on the third attempt he caught it and connected it to the ring in the middle of the escape hatch. Slowly and carefully he was brought up again.

Inside the *Squalus*, the crew had been thrilled to hear the diver's leaden boots on the hull above them. All the men were feeling ill by this time; apart from the numbing cold the amount of oxygen in the air had fallen to a very low level. This was causing sickness, throbbing headaches and aching limbs, the first sign of carbon-dioxide poisoning. They knew that they would soon drift into unconsciousness but now that the bell was definitely on its way it gave them courage to hang on to their lives for a little longer.

Most of the men had seen the rescue chamber before because it was part of their training. Now they could not think about anything else. They remembered it looking like a giant steel egg-cup turned upside down. It was about 10 feet high and 7 feet across and had a central room into which the operators and the passengers were squeezed. Below that it had a sort of metal skirt that fitted over the submarine escape hatch. This 'skirt' could then be pumped free of water so that the submariners underneath could open the hatch and pass through into the bell. It was hauled down to the submarine on a cable by a winch that worked on compressed air. It sounded simple enough but all crossed their fingers and hoped it would work.

As the diving bell was lowered at 11.30 AM, the weather fortunately improved and the sea became as calm as a millpond. The operators of the chamber in its first real test were John Mihalowski and Walter Harmon. Momsem had given them instructions to take on only seven men in the first load in order to see how the bell would behave.

Naquin had been told to select the seven men for the trip to the surface and apart from an officer called Nichols, whom he wanted on top to give information, he chose the men who seemed to be in the weakest condition. Soon after 12 o'clock the rescue chamber settled comfortably over the escape hatch and its lower compartment was emptied of sea water. Then the two hatches leading into the submarine were opened.

The first thing that the submariners felt was the clean, fresh air pouring down to them through the rescue chamber and its air line. They filled their aching lungs with it and at once began to revive like fish put back into water. There were no cheers or shouts for the long-awaited sight of their saviour, in the shape of Mihalowski peering down with a worried smile. It was just too much for them.

Hot coffee, sandwiches and more tins of the carbon-dioxide absorbent were passed down to the ones who were staying behind and the chosen seven were helped into the bell. After this more fresh air was pumped into the forward torpedo room and after about fifteen minutes of preparation the seal was broken with the submarine and the bell rose slowly to the surface. Nichols was the first man out and as he took his first stumbling steps on to *Falcon*'s deck a cheer went up from the fleet of little boats who had been anxiously awaiting this moment for hours. Just to see this handful of men pulled from the grip of the sea made all their efforts worthwhile.

At 3 PM the chamber came back and took a further nine men and three hours later it took nine more. Of the original thirty-three only Naquin and seven others were now left in the submarine. This time Momsem had changed Harmon for another diver called McDonald. As the bell slipped beneath the waves for the last time Momsem, pleased with the ease of the mission up to now, reckoned that the rescue should be over by 9 PM. This might only just be in time as the weather was rapidly worsening and already it was getting dark. The last dive was the smoothest so far; according to Navy tradition Naquin, being the captain, was the last to climb out and he sadly secured the escape hatch on his unfortunate ship *Squalus* for the last time.

The rescue bell lifted off *Squalus* and rose slowly to ·

the surface. It was still 160 feet away, when with a bone-shattering jolt the chamber stopped. Somehow the cable had become jammed. The men were left hanging between the surface and the ocean floor, almost between life and death – it was a nasty moment. The only thing to do was to wind them back down to the sea bed whilst the divers tried to untangle the cable. The diver had so much trouble with it that he finally had to cut the cable completely. This meant that the chamber was now swinging free and had to be hauled up by winches on to the deck of the *Falcon*. As it once more began to climb slowly to the surface the men were horrified to see strands of the wire cable suddenly start to break and unravel.

No chances could be taken on letting the cable break completely or it would be the end for the diving bell and the men inside, so once more Naquin and his ill-fated crew were bumped down to the bottom. Divers were sent down to try and shackle a completely new cable on to the rescue chamber. The pressure of water on the divers' bodies 200 feet down together with severe cold and darkness made it an impossible task. By midnight, with the rescue bell still on the bottom, Momsem recalled the divers and gave up the idea. There was only one slim chance left for them to take. They would haul up the chamber by hand on the damaged cable and hope that it would not snap before it reached the surface.

It was a slow and nerve-racking business but it did work and at half past midnight, the last of the cold, exhausted crew of the *Squalus* staggered out on to the deck of *Falcon* from death into life.

The story of *Squalus* and its happy outcome is a

credit to the US Navy. From start to finish it was a well-organized operation that owed everything to the coolness and clear thinking of the officers in charge and the determination and courage of the divers. However, the most fortunate factors were probably the horizontal positioning of the *Squalus* and the good weather that lasted throughout the actual diving. If the *Squalus* had not settled in such a good position or if the weather had been worse it could have been an entirely different story.

Chapter 4

Disaster in Liverpool Bay

By 1939 submarines had become very respectable. They had proved their worth in World War I and were now a recognized part of almost every navy's fleet. The cliffhanger story of *Squalus* and its eventual happy ending came to the attention of the world. It was an amazing story about brave and determined men which caught everybody's imagination and at the same time left them very disturbed!

Here was a brand-new safely designed submarine which through some small, unexplained defect had plummeted to the bottom of the sea, leaving her well-trained crew helpless to save themselves. Everyone thought there could only be a million-to-one chance of anything similar happening again. Perhaps that was why no one was prepared when it did. The British Navy began sea trials with their T-class submarine *Thetis* on the first day of June 1939, only eight days after the sinking of *Squalus*.

Thetis was one of Britain's latest patrol-type submarines recently completed at the Cammell Laird shipyard in Birkenhead. At 275 feet she was shorter than the *Squalus* by 40 feet, and several hundred tons lighter. At 9.40 AM, in brilliant sunshine, the *Thetis* sailed off down the Mersey and out into Liverpool Bay.

The trials of this submarine were more festive than usual as it was the first time that Cammell Laird had built a submarine of such an important class at their shipyard. Naturally they wanted to celebrate. So, along with the normal crew of 53 carried by a submarine of this size, 50 passengers were aboard. This made a total of 103 people on board, twice the number it had been built for.

These extra passengers, along with observers from Cammell Laird, were important men in the submarine world – officers from other submarines, officials from the Admiralty in London, and senior officers from the flotilla that *Thetis* would join at the end of her trials. All in all it was a very crowded submarine and the compartments seemed to be jammed with people.

In spite of the crush everyone enjoyed the delicious lunch provided by Cammell Laird. It was a perfect June day and the captain, crew and passengers intended to have an enjoyable trip.

The *Thetis* was followed out to sea by the tug *Grebecock* who was supposed to take off any of the passengers not wishing to stay on board when the submarine commenced diving. However, at 1.30 PM the *Grebecock* was told by megaphone, not unexpectedly, that the guests had all decided to stay on board for the trials and the *Grebecock* would only be needed as an observer. So the tug took up a position half a mile to port to watch the *Thetis* dive.

All the usual preparations were made; hatches were closed, diving planes were set and the main ballast tanks were flooded. Everything was ready for an easy gentle dive. With the weight of fifty extra passengers it should

not have been difficult. Surprisingly, however, the
Thetis continued to travel calmly along the surface as if
nothing had happened. The captain, Lieutenant-Commander Guy Bolus filled all the additional ballast tanks
and tried every trick he knew to get the reluctant submarine below the surface. Almost an hour later she was
clearly winning, having only slid a few feet into the
water. It was an embarrassing situation!

Lieutenant Woods, the torpedo officer, worried that
the trouble might be in his department, hurried along to
check the torpedo tubes. The *Thetis* had six of these
built into her bow. They normally held heavy torpedoes
ready to be shot out into the water like bullets when
their outside doors were opened. On trial runs like this,
of course, torpedoes were left behind. When submarines
had difficulty in submerging, the empty torpedo tubes
were sometimes filled with water and used as ballast
tanks. As they each held about 800 lbs of sea water, it
could make quite a difference to whether the submarine
dived or not.

The inside doors of the torpedo tubes looked like
large flat dustbin lids. They could be tested for the presence of water by a little stopcock which spouted water
out through the door if the tube was full. The notes on
the torpedo tubes, passed on from the builders at Cammell Laird, said that tubes 1 to 4 were empty and tubes 5
and 6 had been filled with water as ballast. This had all
been done before *Thetis* left the boatyard.

As the boat was still no nearer to diving, Woods and
another seaman decided to check the tubes. They tested
the stopcock of No 1. No water spurted out, so they
opened the door and found what they expected – an
empty, dry, torpedo tube. They went along in this

manner, finding all the tubes empty until they reached
Nos 5 and 6 which were supposed to be full. A small
amount of water dripped through No 6 stopcock as if
there was at least a little water in there but even after
several checks nothing at all spurted or even trickled out
of No 5's stopcock! Was this the oversight that was
preventing *Thetis* from diving? To Woods it seemed the
probable answer.

There was another type of drain hole on the torpedo
door that Woods could have tested but as he had no
reason to mistrust the stopcock and he was anxious to
help the *Thetis* begin her trials, he ordered the seaman
to open the door of No 5 torpedo tube. The order was
never properly carried out for as the sailor gradually
turned the large lever round to 'open' – the door was torn
out of his hands and the full force of the sea leapt into
the submarine! Not only was the stopcock faulty (it was
later found to have been clogged with paint) but the
outer torpedo door had also been left wide open to the
sea!

Commander Bolus was in the control room still
trying to get the *Thetis* to dive when No 5 torpedo tube
flew open. Now, of course, he had no problem! The bow
of the *Thetis* dipped with a suddenness that threw everyone off balance. Even without the painful pressure he
now had on his eardrums, Bolus would have realized
something pretty serious was wrong. Loud shouts
echoed through the ship: 'Blow main ballasts! Hard to
rise!'

Everything was working in reverse, like a bad dream.
The stubborn *Thetis* that had refused to dive now just
could not stop. Her heavy nose carried her straight to
the bottom where it buried itself in the mud leaving the

rest of the boat swaying at an uncomfortable angle above it.

At the first rush of water Woods acted quickly. He pushed the other man out of the torpedo room and they both heaved the watertight door uphill to close it as Maness had done only the week before in *Squalus*. Unfortunately, this was a different type of door with a large number of fastening clips. In the resulting confusion caused by the fierce onrush of water only one of the clips was screwed up before Woods ordered the men to get behind the next watertight door and made sure of shutting that. He was afraid that water might reach the third compartment in which the batteries were housed.

Unluckily the clip did not hold as he had hoped and in a very short time the two forward compartments were completely flooded. This extra flooded compartment made all the difference. It might be possible to get a submarine back to the surface with one flooded compartment but the weight of two made it out of the question. After Bolus had inspected the ship he took stock of the situation; there were only two courses open to him. He could either attempt a mass escape by means of the breathing sets on board (called Davis Submerged Escape Apparatus) or he could send someone into the flooded compartments through the escape hatch to shut No 5 torpedo tube and open the drain valves. If the latter was successful, the waterlogged compartments could be pumped dry from the main control room and the submarine might surface normally.

Bolus was reluctant to try the first method because some of the passengers had not been trained to use DSEA sets and as the *Thetis* would not be missed for several hours there would be no one on the surface to rescue them. The second possibility seemed to be the best and there was certainly no shortage of volunteers. This scheme had, however, one major drawback: the man who attempted it would not only be subjected to at least fifteen minutes, possibly a lot longer, of extreme cold, but he would also have the weight of 160 feet of water pressing down on him.

This weight of water, about 70 lb all over the body, caused extreme discomfort and pain. Only a very fit, determined person would be able to stand it. The first man who tried had had enough before the escape chamber was even flooded and had to be helped out almost fainting. Two people tried the escape chamber the next time, one of them being Woods, the torpedo officer. He withstood the pressure of water very well but unfortunately his partner collapsed and once more the chamber had to be drained. Woods, who still felt fit, tried once more with another volunteer but the same thing happened. Although Woods was all right the pain for the other man was unbearable!

These attempts to enter the flooded compartments had already taken up three hours of the precious time they had left to make their escape. As it now seemed unlikely that the attempt would work, Bolus decided to abandon the plan and think of something better. It was now 7 PM and there would only be one or two hours of light upon the surface. Had their whereabouts been discovered yet? Would anything be done for them, as it had for the men in the *Squalus*? Should they try to escape now? Commander Bolus called a conference in the officers' wardroom.

The crew of the *Grebecock* had not been very happy about *Thetis*' first dive, particularly as it happened with alarming suddenness after almost an hour with no success. Their job, however, was not to reason why, but merely to follow the *Thetis* and protect her from being rammed accidentally by passing ships. 'New submarines always have minor defects first time out,' the men said to each other uneasily. 'They are probably putting it right underwater.' Commander Bolus had fastened a red flag to his periscope so that *Grebecock* could tell where *Thetis* was from time to time. Everyone kept a sharp lookout for a flash of red but the surface of the sea was strangely still and as time dragged by the *Grebecock*'s crew began to despair of ever seeing the flag again.

The submarine lieutenant on board *Grebecock* as an observer, began to be extremely anxious by 4 PM and sent off a simple warning message to the headquarters at Gosport. He did not want to alarm anyone in case plans had been changed, so the message just said, 'What is the duration of *Thetis*' dive?'

Unfortunately, the *Grebecock* had no direct contact with Gosport so her message would have to follow the same route as a GPO telegram. Everything possible went wrong on the way including a puncture in the telegraph boy's bicycle tyre and it was 6.15 PM before the telegram reached Gosport. By this time, of course, headquarters were already concerned about *Thetis* as she should, by now, have completed her diving trials and reported back to them. With the arrival of the telegram their fears were confirmed. At 6.20 PM the search began.

The first vessel in the area was the destroyer HMS *Brazen*. A flotilla of eight other destroyers was also on its way, two submarines, the salvage ship *Vigilant* and the Navy's submarine rescue ship, *Tedworth*, manned by the best divers in the Navy. The snag was that most of them were still three or four hundred miles away.

The Royal Air Force was called in to comb as much of the area as possible before nightfall and at 9.25 PM one of them spotted the *Thetis'* marker buoy. By a stroke of sheer bad luck the excited navigator took an incorrect bearing which was passed on to the *Brazen*. She spent the whole night searching some miles away from the correct place.

Inside the *Thetis* there was already a great deal of discomfort with far too many people breathing far too little air. The submarine had been overcrowded to begin with but now with the air becoming sour and stale, the atmosphere was overpowering. The gay lunch supplied by Cammell Laird was now just a memory. There would be no more meals because the emergency food supplies lay under water in the flooded compartments.

As a result of Commander Bolus' discussion with the other submarine officers, it had been decided to wait to be rescued although at that moment there was no sign of any rescue ship. But to leave the submarine via an escape compartment, only to drown in a dark empty sea, was not an idea they thought worth considering. In any case many of the submarine's passengers were not young men and the pressure of the water and the coldness of the sea might prove too much for them even if there were rescue ships nearby.

The only positive action they could take would be to make the stern lighter by pumping water from the aft tanks into the forward tanks. This would cause the stern of the submarine to rise nearer to, if not actually above,

the surface of the water. It would make things uncomfortable on board as the angle would be so steep but
if the stern was actually out of the water it would give
them a much better chance of being found. It was in this
position with 18 feet of stern towering up from the
waves and only the little red buoy for company that the
Brazen found her at 7.30 AM the next morning.

It had been a long night in the *Thetis*. Almost all the
men were now forced to lie down as the lack of air made
them so dizzy and weak. Most of them had severe headaches and felt very sick due to increasingly large
amounts of carbon dioxide being created by so many
people exhaling. Conditions were worsening very
quickly now and there was still no sign of rescue. Bolus
then decided that even though it might be too late for the
majority to brave the cold sea, the ones who were young
and fit enough should be given their chance to escape.

He chose two people to make the first attempt: Captain Oram, the head of *Thetis*' flotilla, and the torpedo
officer, Lieutenant Woods. These two were selected as
being the ones with the greatest knowledge of the situation aboard the *Thetis*. It was hoped that when they
were picked up they could assist with the rescue operations. A plan had been devised by the senior submarine
officers as to how the bow could be pumped dry and both
men were to have a copy of this strapped to their wrists
in waterproof containers to hand over when they were
picked up.

Their escape was the first thing that had gone right
since *Thetis* was launched. The two men arrived on the
surface at the same time as the *Brazen* anchored nearby
and they were picked up immediately. Although
severely shocked by the cold they were able to tell of the

ghastly conditions aboard the *Thetis* and how important
a speedy rescue was. They also said that Bolus intended
sending people out of the escape hatches two at a
time.

Although everyone waited anxiously it was two and a
half hours later when two more survivors appeared
and they were picked up immediately. Apparently,
after Oram and Woods left, four people had entered the
escape chamber to speed things up but due to one of
them panicking they had all lost their breathing sets and
drowned. This had been the final blow to the courage of
the men below and no one else felt like trying. The
carbon dioxide in the air was making everyone drowsy.
Many of the older men were already unconscious, bal-
ancing on the thin line between life and death.

The second pair of survivors, a young, strong stoker
and one of Cammell Laird's engine fitters, had been
very lucky to get out when they did. The poisoned air
was making it impossible for men to think clearly
enough to work the machinery of the escape chamber. It
was not surprising then that there were no other heads
bobbing up to the surface of the sea, although there
were occasional bubbles and sounds of hammering.

The survivors grew impatient and terribly anxious:
'What plans are being made to get them out?' they
asked. 'They won't be able to do any more to help themselves, what are you going to do about it?' With no
senior submarine officer on the scene, no destroyers, no
divers, no precious air lines or blow torches there was
no answer to that question although it certainly de-
served one. Where were all these people and equipment,
anyway?

The eight brand-new destroyers appeared forty

minutes later looking impressive and beautiful but particularly useless in this sort of situation. The special rescue vessel *Tedworth* with her expert divers was waiting at a coal yard for fuel 190 miles away so she was not going to be much use. No one had thought about using aeroplanes to fly any of the divers or valuable equipment to the scene.

The greatest tragedy about the whole affair was that no one had been prepared for an accident, even though *Squalus* had been a warning that things do not always go well with new submarines. There were no tough, experienced submariners on hand like Cole, Momsem and McCann; in fact, the *Thetis* had no one to act in her interests until it was too late. The brand-new *Thetis* and her ninety-nine men were dying!

As the day wore on, various ideas were suggested for opening up the stern that still protruded like a headstone from the water. None of them was successful. Finally at 3 PM on June 2nd whilst the *Vigilant* was hauling on the *Thetis'* precarious stern to steady her for another attempt with cutting torches, she twisted herself free. With a deep sigh, as if her patience had finally been exhausted, she slid from view for the last time and with only the red buoy left as a reminder it was as if she had never been.

At 4 o'clock on the 3rd, forty-eight hours after she had sunk, the Admiralty announced to a shocked world that all hope for those on board must be abandoned.

There is a sequel to the Thetis tragedy. Several months later on October 23rd, the *Thetis* was brought to the surface and her dead were put to rest. She was repainted, given a new crew and a new name, HMS *Thunderbolt*. By this time World War II had begun and she was given a lot of useful work to do. She embarked on many missions and saved many lives during the dark years of war. After the lingering memory of her first dreadful day at sea she was finally accepted as a happy, reliable submarine.

In March 1943 she died again. After sinking an enemy steamer out of a large convoy she was depth-charged by an Italian escort ship. Once more she went to the bottom, taking a crew of sixty with her. This time the water was 3,000 feet deep and she did not come up again. Hope for the *Thetis/Thunderbolt* and her crew was once more abandoned.

Chapter 5

The U-Boat Peril

Due north of the most northerly tip of the Scottish main-land, a few miles off John O'Groats, lies a small group of windswept islands called the Orkneys. Today most people only hear about them on radio weather forecasts to shipping in that area. They are bleak islands, desolate and forbidding for most of the year, surrounded by stormy seas and blown on by fierce winds. During two World Wars they were very important to the British Navy.

The islands are arranged like a large necklace around a central bay called Scapa Flow which the British used as a safe anchorage for their Home Fleet. During World War I this harbour was challenged by two U-boats but both were sunk with a loss of all hands in the approaches to Scapa Flow.

When Germany began to invade other European countries in 1939, war broke out again between Germany and Great Britain. Hitler, who was the German leader, appointed the World War I submarine ace, Karl Doenitz, as commander of the submarine section of the German Navy.

Doenitz, convinced that U-boats had a most import-ant part to play in the battles ahead, asked for 300 to be

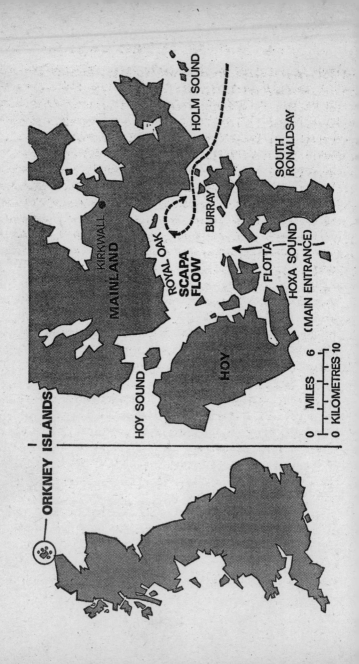

built. However, by the time war had been declared, only
fifty-six had been completed. Doenitz was determined to
use them to the best advantage, however, and decided to
try a sneak attack on the British Home Fleet. He knew
that the British, being drawn into the war unexpectedly,
would have had no chance to change or improve any of
the defences left from the last war twenty years ago.
Aerial photographs also supported this opinion. A
secret U-boat attack just might work – it was certainly
worth trying.

There were seven inlets into the bay, all of which had
booms or various other blockages placed in the entrance
to keep out intruders. Between the islands the current
was also very strong. It was just possible that a cool-
headed U-boat commander could pass through the eastern approach called Holm Sound and from there slip
into the narrow passage of Kirk Sound. This would take
him into Scapa Flow itself. It would be a difficult
mission but if it succeeded the U-boat could do a great
deal of damage.

Doenitz obviously had to take great care to choose
the right man for this job and after a lot of thought
he decided on Gunther Prien, the captain of U-47, and
called him for an interview. To be singled out for such
a task was the highest compliment he could be paid.
For Prien, whose life had already been packed with
adventure, this was the highlight.

As a child he had thought of nothing but the sea and
the great seafarers. Vasco da Gama was his special hero
and he had read his life story over and over again.
Prien's widowed mother was extremely poor and although sorry to lose him was proud when, at fifteen, he

was accepted by the Seamen's College in Finkenwarder in 1923.

Three months later Prien passed his examinations and tried to join a ship. Times were hard in the German Merchant Navy in those days and he had great difficulty in finding a ship to take him. Finally he was taken on by the *Hamburg* as a cabin boy but without wages.

It was very hard work, mostly concerned with looking after the *Hamburg*'s twenty-eight sails. The main mast was 160 feet high and the boys were expected to scramble up and down the rigging in icy winds and rain. The food was poor and the cabin boys were treated very badly. However, it did nothing to destroy Prien's love of the sea. After a couple of months the *Hamburg* was caught in a terrific storm off Ireland and wrecked on the rocks. It was terrifying for young Prien, especially when the crew realized that even the rats were jumping off the ship. They all expected to drown but fortunately the Kingstown lifeboat came out and rescued them.

A few weeks later he signed on another ship, the *Pfalzburg*, a large freighter bound for South America. His day's routine on the freighter was extremely boring as all he did all day was scrub the rust off the metal parts of the ship and repaint it when it needed it. Hardly what he expected when signing on as a sailor!

Unlike most of the deck hands he was serving an apprenticeship at sea or 'working his ticket' in order to become an officer one day. He could not make mistakes or complaints and this made him unpopular with some of the crew and occasionally he was drawn into fights. It was not a very happy time for Prien but, a quiet, determined man, he worked his way up the ladder first by becoming a ship's 'mate' and then by getting his wireless operator's certificate. In January 1932 he took and passed his captain's examinations.

Unfortunately, 1932 also brought lack of work and money to Germany. Prien spent a month in Hamburg trying to get on a ship but he found it impossible. Eventually with no money left and a feeling of failure he went home to the mother he had left nine years before. He tried to get a job in his home town but there were no jobs of any sort – everyone was out of work.

After some weeks he managed to join a Nazi labour camp in Voglsberg some way from his home. His day started at 5.30 AM and finished at 5.30 PM. It was hard outdoor work in all weathers but Prien in his usual calm manner made the best of it and before the year was out reached the high position of camp leader. In January 1933 he heard a rumour that the German Navy was strengthening its ranks and giving jobs to merchant seamen. So once more he went back to sea, but not as a captain because his examinations were worthless in this Navy. He started at the bottom again as an ordinary seaman.

After his period of normal training he was sent to the U-boat training school at Kiel and after some weeks of classwork he went for his first trip in a U-boat. He was fascinated by this amazing machine and was thrilled when at the end of his training he was appointed first officer on the U-26. He enjoyed his work on the U-26 and in the autumn of 1938 he was given his first command.

The day he boarded his shining new boat was a proud one for Prien. This was the goal for which he had always been aiming. Now he had thirty-eight men under his command, mostly young volunteers looking for a more exciting life than they might get on a battleship. The summer of 1939 was a happy time for Prien and his crew as they spent the sunny months practising mock battles in the Atlantic.

Everything changed in August when war was declared. For the crew of the U-47 the hunt was on! The British began to send its merchant ships in armed convoys and the U-boat commanders had instructions to torpedo without warning any ship in such a convoy. Already the war had made people cruel and there was fierce competition between the U-boat crews as to who could sink the most ships in the shortest time. As usual Prien's name came well to the fore in this deadly competition and his actions brought him to the notice of his senior officers.

On Sunday, October 1st, 1939, he was invited to attend an interview in Admiral Doenitz's quarters. Prien was worried when he was sent for because an interview with an admiral on a Sunday afternoon was most unusual. Also present at the briefing was Lieutenant Wellmar, captain of the U-16, which had recently been spying on the British Fleet's defences.

Doenitz asked Wellmar to describe to Prien what he had found out about Scapa Flow's defences. Doenitz then listened whilst the captain of the U-16 gave Prien details of every blockship placed in Scapa Flow's entrances. When Wellmar had finished the admiral stared searchingly into Prien's face and said, 'In spite of this we still think a skilful U-boat commander could squeeze his boat through just here.' He stuck the point of his compass into Kirk Sound on the map. 'What do you think, Prien?'

Prien's head was spinning; he stared back at Doenitz in dumb amazement. Fortunately, a reply was not necessary.

'I hope you understand what I want you to do,' Doenitz went on. 'You do have a choice; think it over and let me know by Tuesday.'

Prien picked up the charts, clicked his heels, saluted, cried 'Heil Hitler' and left the room. Although torn between fear and excitement, he knew there was only one answer he could give!

That evening he spent several hours studying the maps carefully. There was indeed a possible entry in the Kirk Sound passage, a gap between the shore and a group of old concrete-filled ships sunk by the British. Unfortunately it was only about 50 feet wide and 20 feet deep. It would require perfect navigation and a great deal of luck to get through. Prien was doubtful about his chances but would not consider refusing. He reported back to Doenitz the next day and accepted the task.

It was important that the U-47 was put into tip-top working order before setting out. Once this was taken care of a date had to be fixed according to the phase of the moon and the time of the flood tide in the passageway. The darker the night and the more water in the passageway, the better Prien's chances of getting through. The date of departure was finally fixed for October 8th.

It was an unusually clear day for October. The sun glinted faintly on the still, grey hull of the U-47 and there was an autumn nip in the air. Prien stood on the pier above the little submarine looking thoughtfully down at her. The crew were already on board and the U-47 was a hive of bustling activity. From the engine rooms to the galley the men were preparing for the long trip ahead – with an unknown destination. Prien was strangely reluctant to climb on board and take that first step towards glory – or death?

At 10 A M he boarded the U-47 and within seconds the throbbing of the diesel engines echoed round the quiet harbour. The submarine slipped slowly down the Kiel Canal and then out into the grey North Sea. For five days the U-47 pushed onwards, keeping to the surface except when she caught sight of any other ships. The sky became overcast and it began to drizzle. As the journey continued, the men, worn down by the constant smell of diesel oil and the cramped conditions, became bored and irritable. Normally on a trip like this there was the excitement of a chase or an attack on an enemy convoy. This time, in spite of several traces of smoke on the horizon, their commander showed no interest or made any attempt to alter his course. The men were puzzled but said nothing.

By October 12th the weather had become very menacing and the winds were now at gale force. That evening at dusk, Prien stood in the conning tower with Endrass, his executive officer. It was completely dark. Not even a star could be seen through the drizzling rain. Gradually on the port side of the ship, a shadow appeared only slightly deeper than the darkness around them. A sudden thrill of fear shot through Prien; it must be them – the Orkneys and the enemy!

Endrass turned towards his captain and shouted into the teeth of the gale.

'Are we going into the Orkneys, sir?'

'We are going into Scapa Flow,' Prien replied. Whatever Endrass must have felt at that moment, he managed a firm reply.

'That will be fine, sir!'

Prien gave orders for the ship to turn east, so that they would be out of sight of the island, and then to be taken to the bottom.

As they slipped into the depths of the sea the difference between the raging of the winds and the complete stillness on the ocean floor was a great relief for everyone. At 4 AM the crew gathered together in the 'forrard' mess. Prien told them in a matter-of-fact way of his plan to enter Scapa Flow the next day. He then went on to give them their instructions for the hours ahead.

Everyone would now go to their bunks and sleep. At 2 PM (14.00 hours) the cook would be woken by the man on watch. At 4 PM (16.00 hours) dinner would be eaten, after which there would be no more hot food, only chocolate and sandwiches, for as long as the mission lasted. During the mission itself complete silence was to be maintained.

The crew were then dismissed to sleep – not an easy thing after such a piece of news. Prien himself found it impossible. After lying in his bunk for a time going over in his mind their route to the islands, he had to get up. The tension was affecting the whole boat. As he passed through the crew's quarters men tossed and turned in their bunks and in the wardroom the navigator was already poring over the maps. They were soon joined by Endrass, who had also found it impossible to sleep, and the three of them checked and rechecked the charts, memorizing everything they needed to know.

At 4 PM they all sat down to a good meal of veal cutlets and cabbage. After the tables had been cleared away preparations were made for the battle ahead. Charges were fixed to blow up the boat in case it should fall into the hands of the enemy, lifejackets and escape hatches were inspected, and finally the navigator set his course.

At 7 PM the sleeping boat sluggishly lifted itself out of the mud and rose gradually towards the surface. 'Up periscope,' said Prien quietly, and scanned around in a complete circle. Once again it was dark and the sea appeared to be empty. 'Surface,' he called. The little submarine surfaced, the hatches were opened and the welcome fresh air rushed through the boat. Up on the bridge there was nothing to see or hear except the waves breaking against the U-47. Even the wind seemed to have disappeared.

Prien and his officers were standing on the bridge gratefully breathing in the fresh air when they suddenly realized that the sky was getting lighter. Behind the clouds pointed rays of light began to flicker and sparkle like some far-away firework display. Fear clutched at Prien's stomach. For the first time he was really frightened. This was completely unexpected – it was the Aurora Borealis or the Northern Lights!

They had counted on a dark moonless night for their attack but now the boat had a much greater chance of being seen and the mission stood in great danger. Prien hesitated, wondering whether he should go ahead or wait. He decided to go ahead, in spite of his doubts. He ordered a new course to be set and had the engines turned to half-speed ahead. A new thought occurred to him. It was Friday the 13th!

As they cautiously drew nearer to the islands the engines of the U-47 sounded unusually loud in the deep silence. Prien trained his binoculars anxiously at the land looking for the opening that his map told him should be there – Kirk Sound. It was!

'Left full rudder,' he ordered. 'New course will be west.'

At 12.15 AM the U-47 turned into Kirk Sound and began to manoeuvre towards the sunken hulks that blocked it. Straight away they began to feel the pull of the treacherous current that flowed around the islands, pulling them urgently towards the waiting hulks. Prien continued to shout instructions to the helmsman and, working skilfully as a team, they managed to get the boat into the narrow channel between the blockships and the land.

Suddenly there was an alarming grinding noise on the underside of the boat as it grated against the bottom and a sickening jolt as it became entangled in a cable from one of the sunken ships. Prien had to move quickly from side to side so that he could see what needed to be done. Somehow they worked their way free and then, as suddenly as it had come, the current was gone and the whole wide bay of Scapa Flow opened up in front of them. It was still and calm and the beautiful Northern lights were reflected in it like a giant mirror. Prien held his breath and then said quietly, 'We are inside!' It was now 12.27 AM. Friday the 13th had come and gone.

The U-47 crept forward stealthily towards the middle of the bay. The men on the bridge strained their ears and their eyes for any sign of the enemy. All was quiet, only a few odd lights in sleeping tankers; obviously everyone who anchored here imagined himself to be very safe.

There was nothing to be seen in the southern half of the bay so they turned to the north-east where, according to Doenitz, they would find the main anchorage of the British Fleet. As they crept forward a sight met their eyes that would have terrified lesser men. First of all they saw the towering shadow of the mighty battleship *Royal Oak* – the prize they most desired. Behind her was another battleship that looked very much like the *Repulse*. There were also several destroyers close by. Prien felt like a fox who had sneaked into a yard full of sleeping chickens!

He decided to attack the *Repulse* first because, as they were so near to the *Royal Oak*, she would be a certain target. Prien gave instructions for the first torpedo to be aimed at the *Repulse*'s bow and the other three for the starboard side of the *Royal Oak*.

'All tubes ready,' Prien's command rang out. The reply came back,

'Tube one, ready.'

'Tube one, fire!' Prien shouted.

The torpedo shot from the U-47 leaving a trail of white bubbles in its rear. A dull blast reached back to the submarine closely followed by a spout of water. 'Second tube, ready,' called up the torpedo crew. Speed was now very important. It was a terrifying moment as they turned to face the *Royal Oak*, torpedoes ready to fire. How could anything disturb this sleeping giant?

The remaining three torpedoes were fired into the side of the mighty ship. Prien watched fascinated as the trails of bubbles travelled every second nearer to her hull. He waited breathlessly until the bubbles had long disappeared. Absolutely nothing happened! The mighty battleship still slumbered on undisturbed. There was no sign of life on her decks, no lights, no shouting voices – nothing!

To Prien it seemed like a bad dream. How could three torpedoes have missed at this close range? He could only imagine that the batch of torpedoes must have been faulty. Sick with disappointment he made ready to dive and make his escape as quickly as possible before he was set upon by the destroyers. Looking around, however, it occurred to him that in spite of all they had done, no one had noticed their presence in the bay! There was no sign of life anywhere!

Hardly believing their luck he cried, 'Reload the torpedo tubes!' Prien stood on the bridge, tense and watchful. In the bottom of the boat the crew wrestled with the heavy, greasy 18-foot-long torpedoes, pushing and heaving them into the empty tubes in the bow.

Unable to wait for four to be refilled Prien called a halt when three were ready – it was by now 1.15 AM and Prien could stand the strain of waiting no longer.

Once again he lined up his shots, once again he watched the trail of bubbles leading towards the *Royal Oak*. This time he was rewarded by a different sight. One of the torpedoes had hit the big ship's magazine room where all her explosives were stored. A gigantic explosion split the great ship in half. Within seconds the U-47 was being bombarded with huge pieces of wreckage which were falling from the sky like hailstones. Prien was rooted to the spot by this spectacular sight and had great difficulty in tearing his eyes away from it long enough to shout down to the crew waiting impatiently beneath him.

'She's finished!'

The crew responded with triumphant cheers.

After the flames of the explosion had died down, Prien saw that the *Royal Oak* was listing badly to starboard and decided that it was time for the U-47 to make herself scarce. He swung the boat around until her bow was pointing towards home and ordered full speed on the engines. As they left the scene the wounded giant *Royal Oak* rolled over and gradually slipped into the sea taking to the bottom of the bay 24 officers and 809 men. An evil night's work.

By now the British were seeking revenge and the whole bay had come to life. Every craft in Scapa Flow had been unleashed to search for the invader. Prien, very aware of the trail of bubbles they were leaving behind, felt sure they must be seen! A destroyer suddenly streaked towards them, its headlights piercing and sharp; surely it must have caught their trail?

For the officers on the bridge it seemed as if the submarine was running on the spot. As the U-boat had approached Kirk Sound it had become caught in the current again and was being tossed from side to side. Even with the engines full on, it was getting nowhere. 'Extreme speed ahead!' called down Prien. 'Couple up the electric motors to the diesels. Give her all you've got!'

As the U-47 struggled hopelessly against the swift flow of the current the officers on the bridge saw to their relief that the destroyer had suddenly swept away in a new direction dropping depth-charges all around her. None of them were near enough to affect the U-47 which by now had reached the dangerous shallows of Kirk Sound.

This time Prien tried to manoeuvre between a blockship and the wooden jetty on the southern side. Once again the U-47's keel grinding on the bottom forced them to stop, unable to go backwards or forwards. The crew stood inside the boat, dripping with perspiration. They could imagine the U-47 sitting there high and dry like a fish out of water waiting for the British to come and collect her next morning!

It was a nasty few moments but somehow, with Prien's expert coaxing, she managed to wriggle her way out again without too much damage to the boat. At last there was nothing but the great empty sea in front of them.

By the morning of the 17th the U-47 was chugging back up the Kiel Canal to a jubilant homecoming. Bands were playing and important people were lining the quayside, full of pride and congratulations. Prien and his entire crew were flown to Berlin in Hitler's private plane to receive personal thanks from the leader himself. This was a very proud moment for Gunther Prien, the poor widow's son from Leipzig, who had started his naval career as a cabin boy. Nineteen months later Prien's U-boat failed to return from its last war patrol. His vessel was eventually presumed lost with all hands. Germany mourned the death of the hero of Scapa Flow.

Chapter 6

Human Torpedoes

At the same time as Gunther Prien was dealing a deadly blow to the British Fleet in Scotland, U-boats were also creating havoc amongst British shipping in the Atlantic. These U-boats were sent out alone to search for unescorted ships and in the first four months of the war they found and sank 144 of them. German U-boat factories were now working at full speed and, as the submarines multiplied, Admiral Doenitz, the U-boat supreme commander, devised a new plan.

For safety reasons Britain began sending her ships out in large convoys. Doenitz followed suit and gave orders that his submarines should also operate in groups of ten or twenty. On sighting a British convoy the U-boats would space themselves about a mile apart into a curved egg-shape and submerge. As soon as the unsuspecting convoy had sailed into the formation, the submarines would close their ranks like the jaws of a trap and open their attack. These 'wolf packs', as they became known, were the terror of the seas and in the six months from June to October of 1940 they took a horrifying toll of shipping: some 1,395,000 tons were destroyed. The German U-boat commanders called it their 'happy' time. For the British it meant serious trouble!

Britain's great fleet, thought to be the world's mightiest, was now being reduced with frightening ease. It was a worrying time for the British people and their leaders.

One of the British Navy's most important tasks was to bottle up the new German warships in the North Sea and prevent them from venturing farther afield. This left the British with very few large ships to man other important outposts.

By November 1941 the British Eastern Mediterranean Fleet had only three battleships left. These were the flagship *Barham*, the *Queen Elizabeth* and the *Valiant*. On November 25th, 1941, in broad daylight, a lone German U-boat, quite by chance, sighted the three battleships steaming along in a line. They were protected, as usual, by several escort destroyers. With a suicidal display of reckless courage the U-boat commander drove his boat straight at the *Barham* on a fast collision course, firing four torpedoes as it went.

The battleship was hit in the worst possible place, her magazine room, where tons of explosives were stored. The *Barham* blew up, hurling wreckage everywhere and killing 800 men. In the following confusion the escort destroyers lost the U-boat and she made good her escape.

This tragic loss to the British Fleet forced her to withdraw her last two precious Mediterranean battleships from the high seas and anchor them at the well-guarded harbour of Alexandria. It was intended that they should remain there, carefully wrapped in anti-torpedo nets, only to be brought out when absolutely necessary. The British had reckoned without the fearless cunning of the Italian 10th Light Flotilla!

On June 10th, 1940, almost a year after the beginning of World War II Italy joined forces with Germany and declared war on Britain and France. Italy was a welcome ally for Germany for many reasons, one of which was the secret weapon that the Italian Navy had been developing. It was known as a human torpedo or more familiarly, a 'pigboat'.

For several years Italian engineers had worked on the idea of a destructive weapon that could be launched from a submarine and guided by man into a pre-planned place such as a secret anchorage. Its novelty value and total unexpectedness meant that it could destroy a large amount of enemy shipping, or so the inventors hoped! A man called Paolucci had the idea of swimming from a submarine carrying a weapon of his own invention: a torpedo with a compressed air tank to keep it afloat. For many months he trained at night towing a barrel for practice but finally the Italian Navy persuaded him to join forces with a naval engineer, Major Rosetti, who had been working on a similar device since 1914.

These two men were soon joined by other interested engineers and, after years of trial and error, a new underwater weapon took shape. This machine, although similar in size and shape to a torpedo, was really a miniature submarine. It was driven along by an electric motor and steered by a crew of two with a wheel similar to that of an aeroplane. Its greatest advantage was that instead of being cooped up inside, as in a real submarine, the men sat astride the machine as if they were riding a motor scooter and were protected only by a curved plastic shield.

The riders would obviously have to be excellent underwater swimmers. Wearing breathing apparatus

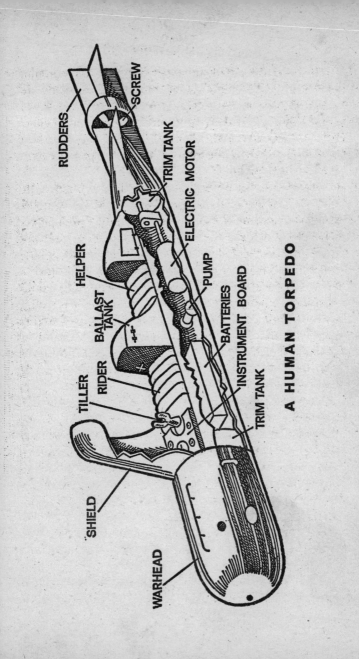

A HUMAN TORPEDO

RUDDERS

SCREW

TRIM TANK

ELECTRIC MOTOR

HELPER

PUMP

BALLAST TANK

BATTERIES

INSTRUMENT BOARD

TILLER

RIDER

TRIM TANK

SHIELD

WARHEAD

they would then be able to move on and off the craft at will, cutting through nets and setting explosive charges. The little machines could travel up to thirty miles and could carry with them very powerful explosives. All the dials were painted in glowing luminous paint so that the divers could navigate their tiny crafts in the dark depths of the sea. In 1936 a small unit was formed called the '10th Light Flotilla'. Four years later when Italy joined the war the Chief of Naval Staff ordered twelve more human torpedoes to be built. Eager young officers seeking adventure were easily recruited and serious training began.

The headquarters of this little band was the Italian submarine *Scire* whose commander was Captain Valerio Borghese. The *Scire* was no ordinary submarine, in fact even her crew were forced to admit that she was the strangest-looking vessel ever to sail the seas. She had been built in the normal way but when she was taken over by the 10th Light Flotilla she had all the guns removed from her decks. These were replaced by three large round containers which were to house the midget submarines.

As she was now unarmed it had been decided to transform her into a peaceful-looking vessel by the clever use of paint. The whole of the *Scire* had been painted pale green, the shade nearest to the colour of the Mediterranean Sea. On each side, in a darker shade of green, was outlined the shape of a fishing trawler. The idea behind this scheme was that anyone sighting the *Scire* on the horizon would be taken in by the disguise and not bother to take a closer look.

The strange thing about this, however, was that the bows of the imitation fishing trawler were pointing in the opposite direction to the bows of the real submarine! Anyone watching the fishing trawler moving along for a minute or so would be rather surprised to see her travelling backwards. Even her captain, Borghese, apparently did not understand this. He thought her the clumsiest-looking ship he had ever seen and said that she was more likely to be taken for a barge than anything else. Despite this the submariners found her a happy, comfortable ship and there were few grumbles.

The *Scire*'s first mission was to Gibraltar on September 21st, 1941. She dropped her crew of torpedo-men with their machines as close to the harbour as she dared. The torpedo-men had a very successful night. They sank three British ships, two of which were valuable oil tankers, and returned to the *Scire* without mishap. Back in Italy the crew of the *Scire* were highly praised for their courage and the torpedo pilots were given silver medals. The new secret weapon had certainly proved itself useful.

It was at this point in the story that the two British battleships *Queen Elizabeth* and *Valiant* were taken into the harbour at Alexandria for their protection. For the 10th Flotilla and their successful new weapon, the battleships were too great a challenge to ignore! The operation on Alexandria was planned very carefully and in absolute secrecy. Aeroplanes photographed the harbour and the position of its berths. Spies were sent out to discover as much as possible about the position of the nets and other obstructions in the mouth of the harbour.

There were three crews of torpedo pilots on board the *Scire*, two men to each machine. On Torpedo 221 rode the leader, De La Penne with his partner Bianchi. On the second machine rode Marcageli and Schergat and the third machine had Montellotta and Marino. All three torpedo crews volunteered for the mission although they had no idea what it was about. They were only told that they must settle their private affairs because if they took part in the mission all they could expect was imprisonment in a war camp or death.

On December 3rd the *Scire* left her home base at La Spezia as if taking part in a routine cruise. The crew of the *Scire* were also kept in the dark about their destination but they had an inkling that it was far more important than usual. There was a certain feeling of tension in the air. After leaving the harbour the *Scire* had a rendezvous with another vessel out at sea. This ship loaded on to the *Scire* the precious containers carrying torpedo machines Nos 221, 222 and 223 which had just been collected from the factory after being overhauled. They also delivered secret packages containing special clothing and breathing apparatus for the torpedo pilots.

The men were delighted at being reunited with their vehicles; each team always used the same torpedo and was aware of any small faults or peculiarities in its handling. Trusting only their own judgement they checked every inch of the machines to be certain they were in tip-top condition.

The long journey then began. The only interesting incident on the way was when the *Scire* saw an enemy submarine sitting quietly on top of the water. The *Scire* first of all sent a friendly signal but received no reply. The Italian commander Borghese was rather worried at this as both submarines were surfaced and the enemy submarine had guns, which put the *Scire* at a

distinct disadvantage. Suddenly the enemy submarine
started to move nearer and eventually joined them sailing a course just alongside. Without making any signal
whatever the strange submarine sailed along with them
for several anxious miles. Then, equally mysteriously, it
turned away and made off at a rapid rate. Perhaps a
close look at a trawler sailing backwards had been too
good to miss! Whatever the reason, the crew of the *Scire*
were glad to see the back of her.

It seemed a long journey, lasting fifteen days altogether, and for the sixty people on board the boat it
became increasingly trying. The crew carried out all
their normal duties but the six torpedo pilots were allowed to spend long days dozing in their bunks and
eating the best food on the ship. The only thing they had
to do was to attend the ship's doctor every day for a
thorough medical. De La Penne, the captain of the torpedo team, had a passion for fruitcake and appeared to
spend the whole of the voyage either nibbling it or sleeping.

On the 16th the *Scire* ran into a heavy storm. For the
next two days Borghese decided to keep the *Scire* on the
bottom, even at night, as too much pitching and rolling
might damage the machines and he did not want to take
any chances with such valuable cargo. Throughout the
day of the 18th the *Scire*, still submerged, drew closer to
Alexandria. They were now travelling through a mined
area of sea so they went down to a depth of 200 feet, to
avoid any traps laid for unwary submarines. The navi-
gators found this a difficult time as it was vital to keep
strictly to the planned route. If, when they arrived at the
harbour, they surfaced only half a mile away from the
right place, the result could be disastrous.

As the *Scire* neared its secret destination, the torpedo-men dressed in their black rubber suits and prepared their machines, ready to be pushed out into an unwelcoming sea. All of them felt the cold fist of fear in their stomachs; they were now fully aware of the difficult task they were expected to carry out. Each team of operators had been ordered to attack a certain ship and had been given information about where to find its moorings.

Somehow, by cutting through the gateway of nets at the mouth of the harbour, each team had to enter and seek out its own personal target. Its first task was to attach the large blocks of explosives carried by the torpedo to the hull of the ship. Then it was to lay a number of incendiary, or fire-spreading, bombs in the harbour timed to go off one hour after the ships exploded. It was hoped that when the ships blew up large amounts of oil and wreckage would spill into the harbour. When the other bombs exploded an hour later they would set fire to this and the flames would eventually spread and destroy not only all the shipping in the harbour but also the warehouses and other important buildings. It was a plan completely without mercy – if it worked, it would spell disaster for the British!

By 6.40 PM when the submarine was about one and a half miles away from the Alexandria breakwater, her engines were cut, and she hung silently below the surface whilst Borghese surveyed the scene through his periscope. It was even darker than they had hoped, not a sign of a light anywhere, and the sea was calm and smooth. As they surfaced, the sinister figures in their shiny black suits stood by their machines thoughtfully. Would they come out of this mission alive? If so, would they ever see their families or their homeland again? 'Commander,' one of them said to Borghese, 'how about giving us a good-luck kick?' Borghese, glad to help in this traditional Italian way, delivered a hard kick to each shiny seat before the men and machines were dropped into the water. He did not envy them their task – they were going to need a lot more than good luck.

It was now up to the *Scire* to make herself as scarce as possible because if she was caught anywhere around it would soon give the game away. She made off under-water at full speed and did not stop or come to the surface for thirty-nine hours. By this time, of course, the whole thing was over.

Meanwhile, back in the harbour the torpedo-men found conditions in the sea far better than they had expected. They had certainly been dropped in a very good position. Already they could make out a few tiny lights and as they approached they saw and heard people talking at the end of one of the piers. Their six heads just above the waterline scanned the gates looking for any hole or gap in the netting. Suddenly, out of the blackness, three enemy destroyers loomed up and stopped right in front of them. The torpedo pilots re-alized that they were queueing up at the harbour en-trance waiting to be let in. As the net gates opened to admit the destroyers the six Italians boldly slipped in behind them and seconds later were inside the inner harbour.

It was, of course, an unbelievable stroke of luck for the torpedo pilots but most of the credit must go to the inventors. Had the British had the slightest idea that

such clever little machines existed they would obviously
have been much more careful about their arrangements
for opening the gate.

With the most difficult part of their mission behind
them, the three teams separated and went about the
business of finding their own ships. De La Penne and
Bianchi were planning to attack the battleship *Valiant*.
Helped by the memory of the aerial photographs of the
moorings it was not long before the massive 32,000-ton
Valiant loomed up in front of them. Without too much
difficulty the team slipped over the top of the *Valiant*'s
anti-torpedo net and manoeuvred their machine alongside. They started to dive under the keel to fix the explosives when, without warning, the tiny submarine
went completely out of control and sank. De La Penne
managed to swim to the surface but Bianchi seemed to
have completely disappeared.

The harbour was still quiet and undisturbed so De La
Penne decided to dive to the harbour bottom and try to
start the torpedo's engine. Looking at it more closely he
realized he was wasting his time: the propeller had
become snarled up with a piece of wire. De La Penne
was furious at being thwarted after getting so near to his
target, and he determined not to give up. The only possible thing he could do was to drag the machine by brute
force until he got it right under the ship. After forty
minutes of heaving and dragging the torpedo through
the sticky mud he thought he would never make it. The
murky water was so stirred-up that he could not see a
thing through his goggles. The strain on his breathing
was so great that he thought his lungs would burst at any
moment.

Then he banged his head on something hard! After

touching it carefully he realized that he had hit the keel of the *Valiant*; obviously she was anchored in a shallower place than they had realized. This gave him new hope and with his last bit of strength he managed to detach the bomb from the torpedo and fasten it to the bottom of the *Valiant*. It was due to go off at 6 AM. De La Penne then surfaced and grabbed off his mask. After a few lungfuls of fresh air he began to feel a great deal better. He began to swim away slowly, not quite sure what to do next, when a sudden burst of machine-gun fire stopped him short.

Clambering on to the *Valiant*'s mooring buoy with a gesture of surrender he was delighted to find his team-mate Bianchi also clinging to it. Apparently, after the torpedo had gone out of control Bianchi had fainted and later came round floating on top of the water. Realizing there was now nothing he could do he had hidden on the marker buoy hoping not to be noticed until the mission was over. The two Italians were taken off the buoy and on to the *Valiant* where they were carefully cross-examined. The British captain soon realized that some sort of charge had been set underneath his ship. In the murky harbour water it would take hours to find it.

The torpedo-men repeatedly refused to give any information and finally they were taken to the depths of the ship and placed in a hold which happened to be very close to where the bomb had been placed. The two brave men sat there quietly whilst the explosives ticked away, practically under their feet. It was 4 AM.

The other two crews had been consistently lucky and their missions had been carried out without a hitch. Both teams sank their machines at the bottom of the harbour. The crew who had laid the charge on the tanker even managed to swim ashore and got as far as the city of Alexandria before being captured. The other crew were spotted swimming away and taken aboard the *Queen Elizabeth*.

Sitting in the hold beside Bianchi, who was still rather ill, De La Penne watched the minutes tick by very slowly. The crew had treated them with respect, even kindness, and he began to feel a heavy responsibility for the hundreds of men aboard the great ship. Destroying a man-of-war was one thing but allowing the lives of all her crew to be taken needlessly was quite another. At ten minutes to six he requested another interview with the captain. He told him that his ship was due to explode within the next few minutes and that it would be a good idea under the circumstances to take the crew off the ship.

As he spoke there was a loud boom from the other side of the harbour which tore a very large hole in the tanker *Sagona* and also damaged the destroyer *Jervis* that was lying next to her. After this the captain of the *Valiant* lost no time in abandoning ship!

A few minutes later when only the captain and a few crew were left behind, the great vessel reared up in the air to the sound of a mighty roar before settling back this time right on the muddy bottom of Alexandria harbour. De La Penne was still on board when it happened but apart from a few grazes was surprised to find himself unhurt. He was standing on the bridge beside the captain when a third explosion marked the passing of the *Queen Elizabeth*. All six torpedo-men survived the explosions and were taken to prisoner-of-war camps. They were kept there until 1944 when Italy was forced to surrender. They then returned to Italy where they were awarded gold medals for gallantry.

This may have been the end of the 10th Flotilla's particular story but surprisingly it was not the end of the British Mediterranean Fleet. Both battleships were badly damaged and put completely out of action. The *Queen Elizabeth*, however, had been in the more fortunate position of being in an even shallower anchorage than the *Valiant*. This meant that even with a hole 40 feet square she only sank into 12 feet of water.

Immediately after the explosion a quick-thinking British Navy had her pushed upright again and her normal routine was carried out just as if nothing had happened. A new waterline was quickly painted in and the ship's carpenters sawed great lengths off the gang planks in order to complete the picture. Next morning the sailors paraded on the deck of the ship under the eye of the Admiral of the Fleet just as if everything was fine. This did not go unnoticed by the Italian aircraft looking over the area and for good measure a photograph was sent to the papers. This clever bluff was completely accepted by the Italians who thought that although the attack on the *Valiant* had been a success the *Queen Elizabeth* was still waiting in the harbour, a threat to their own Navy and ready to pounce when necessary.

Chapter 7

The Unsinkable Tirpitz

Part I – The Unlucky 'Arthur'

The destruction of their battleships was a bitter blow to the British Navy. The incident immediately produced a letter from Mr Winston Churchill, the Prime Minister, to Admiral Max Horton the British submarine chief. He wanted to know why the Royal Navy had no answer to the Italians' clever inventions and suggested that perhaps the British would benefit by copying their ideas.

This letter was the beginning of the 12th Submarine Flotilla, a group formed with the sole intention of taking revenge upon the Germans by attacking their battleships, which were so carefully hidden away in Norway. The pride of the German fleet was the gigantic battleship *Tirpitz* which had taken shelter at the very tip of a Norwegian fiord. (A fiord is a long, narrow arm of sea, usually flanked by high cliffs, stretching right into the heart of the country.) This fiord was too far from British shores to be in range of the Royal Air Force bombers and too shallow for attack by normal-sized submarines.

The destruction of the *Tirpitz* would be a major

victory for the British and it was with this in mind that men began to be recruited and trained to join the 12th Flotilla, the most dangerous section of the British submarine fleet.

British naval engineers were busily searching for an underwater weapon similar to the Italian 'human torpedo' and were already at an advanced stage in the development of a midget submarine known as an X-craft. These little craft were different from the Italian machines in that they were tiny copies of a normal-sized submarine. Unfortunately, because of teething troubles the X-craft were still not ready to be taken to sea in 1942. It was decided that, as a stopgap, a team of human torpedo machines would be quickly built and used until the X-craft were ready. One of the Italian 'pigboats' had been captured by the British and, using this as a basic design the first British version of a human torpedo was soon on the production line.

In the meantime, the flotilla had plenty to do in the way of general training and underwater diving. They were trained by two submarine officers who were experts in submarine warfare, Commanders Sladen and Fell. After the first ten days a wooden dummy was produced to help the men to get the feel of the new weapon. The sailors called it *Cassidy*. Although it had no motor and could not actually move along, it did have ballast tanks to make it sink to the bottom and rise to the surface again. The men could then sit astride it and get used to submerging on this unusual type of vehicle. Unfortunately, on the first day of trials, *Cassidy* was extremely unhelpful and when the ballast tanks were completely filled with water it remained sitting on the surface. It took a great deal of time and several pounds of lead weights before it could be persuaded to leave the safety of the surface and give its riders a taste of undersea life.

It was two months before a real human torpedo was ready so the men had plenty of time to get used to the obstinate *Cassidy* before they were taken off to a secret training base on the island of Lewis in the Outer Hebrides.

In early June the packing-cases arrived carrying the first completed machine or the *Real One* as it soon came to be known. After the first few attempts the crew got the *Real One* performing in a way that *Cassidy* never had. It could dive and surface without any trouble and the crew found the machine very easy to manoeuvre.

The British torpedo boats were nicknamed 'chariots' by the Navy and the first one, at least, was a success. The great drawback about charioteering, as the men soon discovered, was the intense discomfort always experienced in the water. Unlike the lucky Italian torpedomen who worked the warm waters of the Mediterranean, British charioteers had to face the icy cold of the North Sea, which even on the sunniest day is not particularly inviting! The rubber diving suits were painfully tight, especially round the head and ears, and sometimes they leaked. The men's hands, which were left free for dealing with nets and explosives, became cut and swollen with the extreme cold. The breathing gear was difficult to get used to: a rubber mouthpiece had to be clamped between the teeth whilst the nose was pinched by a cruel metal clip. This was bearable for a time but after hours in the water the charioteers had extremely sore gums and noses!

As the rest of the 'real' chariots arrived, work began

in earnest. The charioteers were taught to cut through nets, attack in complete darkness and return to base without being discovered. These 'mock' missions were, on the whole, successful but there were mishaps. Sometimes crewmen disappeared underwater and were found washed up on the rocks, usually still alive but not always. This unnerved everyone and reminded them of the constant danger they were in even when taking part in practice missions.

The main cause of these accidents was the fresh water that trickled down from the mountain streams and into the salt-water lochs. As any experienced swimmer will know, swimming in the sea is always easier than swimming in an indoor pool because the salt in the sea thickens the water and helps to keep you up. The chariots were designed to be used in the sea and so were specially weighted to float or submerge in salt water. If a chariot speeding along smoothly hit one of these patches of thin fresh water it became too heavy and plunged to the bottom like a stone. Often this meant a drop of 100 feet!

The squeezing pressure of water caused great pain to the charioteer's body, particularly the ears, and could result in unconsciousness. With experience the divers learned to cope with the effects of this sudden pressure by opening the valve wider on the oxygen bottle and taking larger gulps of oxygen from it. Repeated swallowing also helped to reduce the pain and discomfort.

By October it was decided that the charioteers were ready for the attempt on *Tirpitz* and after a completely successful mock attack the date was fixed for October 26th. The charioteers and their machines were to be taken to Norway on board an old fishing trawler called

Arthur. False papers had to be prepared for the ship and her crew. She was to become a Norwegian fishing trawler converted into a cargo vessel. To complete the disguise she was to carry a load of peat which she was supposed to be delivering to a port called Trondheim.

A Norwegian named Lief Larsen had been chosen to lead them on this mission and he seemed the ideal man for the job. After escaping from Norway during the German invasion, he worked as a spy for the British Navy posing as the captain of a Norwegian fishing trawler. He organized many trips along the coast of Norway, landing and picking up secret agents and helping the Norwegian Underground movement. Consequently, he knew the coastline like the back of his hand.

Arthur's crossing of the North Sea was not particularly pleasant; the sea was very rough and a lot of the men were sea-sick. No one was sorry when the shores of Norway were sighted on the afternoon of the 28th. They were about twenty miles from the coast when the engines broke down. The whole of Norway was occupied by the Germans so their first concern was to haul the chariots out of sight. They decided to fasten them underneath the hull of the *Arthur* with ropes, but this proved easier said than done, and it was not until the early hours of the following morning that the chariots were secured and the cargo boat able to continue.

Once again there was difficulty with the engines; smoke began to belch out of them and their speed was cut down to half. It became obvious that repairs would be needed. Fortunately Larsen knew of a nearby agent who might help them. The agent, a man named Olavsen, lived at a place on the coast called Hestwick. A Norwegian member of the crew found the man and brought him to the boat. A blacksmith friend of Olavsen's was knocked up in the middle of the night to do the repairs and by 7 AM it was finished. After two hours' sleep the crew were ready to sail again.

Another near-disaster occurred when on a completely calm patch of water they encountered a German patrol boat. The sea was clear and transparent and it seemed impossible that the Germans would not notice the machines slung underneath the fishing smack. They were boarded by German officers who, after examining their papers, wished them a very good day and went on their way.

The *Arthur* continued on until, as darkness fell, it reached the mouth of the fiord which held the *Tirpitz* at its head. The plan was for the *Arthur* to stop at Trondheim, the nearest port to the *Tirpitz* mooring, and under cover of dark unleash the machines which would be mounted and ridden into the attack.

The *Arthur* was just nearing Trondheim when, as it rounded a bend in the fiord, it encountered an unexpectedly strong wind. The charioteers, nearing the beginning of their mission, were already struggling into their rubber suits. With surprising swiftness the weather worsened and the *Arthur* began to lurch and roll. She had entered a particularly bad storm. The keel knocked disturbingly as strong waves took hold of the chariots and hurled them back and forth against the *Arthur*'s hull. With fingers crossed the charioteers continued their preparations down in the bottom of the boat. It would be suicidal to hang around the busy port until the following night. The attack had to take place that night or not at all. There was still another hour before they would have to leave the boat to start the attack and with luck the worst of the storm would be over.

Then suddenly they froze as a rending, groaning noise, gradually becoming louder, filled the ship. The *Arthur* suddenly lurched to one side and with her leapt the hearts of everyone on the ship. One of the chariots must have broken loose and hit the ship's propeller! The captain guided her into a sheltered place and one of the charioteers who was already in diving gear went down to have a look at the damage. He returned to the surface with shocking news; not one but both of the machines were missing. After all their setbacks to get only one hour away from the *Tirpitz* and then find both weapons were lying useless at the bottom of the fiord! The crew of the *Arthur* were sick with disappointment.

Now they had to save themselves. They had no papers for the return journey, the propeller was damaged and the engine was not up to making the long journey home. The only thing to do was to sink the *Arthur* and walk to the border of Sweden which was a neutral country and so not involved in the war. After boring holes in the *Arthur* they left her settling into the water and began their long trek to the border sixty miles away.

They split into two parties, each with a Norwegian leader. They left at separate times and on different routes and it was a cold, wearying journey for both parties. With one exception they all managed to escape. The party commanded by Larsen ran into a German patrol just before crossing the border and one of the British crew members, Evans, was shot and captured. He survived that particular wound but was killed as a spy before the end of the war. Larsen and the rest of the charioteers returned to England within a month, hoping to be given another chance of attacking the *Tirpitz*.

The charioteers never did get that second crack at the *Tirpitz* for soon afterwards they were sent to Malta on a different mission. This time the chariots were taken to their destination, the Sicilian port of Palermo, by the submarines *Thunderbolt* and *Trooper*. It was another stormy night and the crew of the *Thunderbolt* felt uneasy. On nights like this it was difficult to forget that their boat was the refloated *Thetis*. Inside her compartments, however many times she was repainted, the high rusty watermark showing the months she had spent on the sea bottom always showed through. Despite their fears, the mission was to go well.

Two of the teams managed to get inside the harbour and they attacked six ships. A new Italian cruiser and three destroyers were sunk and two merchantmen were badly damaged. It was very encouraging for the 12th Submarine Flotilla but it still left the problem of the *Tirpitz*!

Part II – Midget Submarines

The first X-craft was finally launched on March 15th, 1942, after taking nearly three years to build. The three men who made up her crew were chosen for their experience in normal-sized submarines. They must have been a little worried when they saw their first miniature submarine, the X3! The length of the X3 was about 50 feet, which does not seem very small, but after fitting in such important items as a propeller and rudder it left

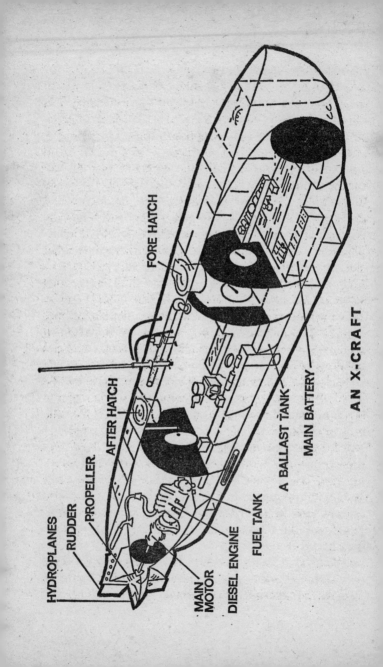

HYDROPLANES
RUDDER
PROPELLER.
AFTER HATCH
FORE HATCH

MAIN
MOTOR
DIESEL ENGINE
FUEL TANK
MAIN BATTERY
A BALLAST TANK

AN X-CRAFT

only 35 feet, about the length of a London bus, for actual living space. Given sufficient height this would have been almost comfortable but as the ceiling was only 5 feet away from the floorboards it made it impossible even to stand in an upright position.

Besides the control room, there were only two main compartments, an engine and battery room and an escape compartment. This room was designed to let the divers get in and out, to cut through nets, lay bombs, and to escape quickly in an emergency. The only thing the X3 lacked were torpedo tubes. These were amply replaced by two large blocks of explosives placed on either side of the torpedo's hull. They were very effective as each contained two tons of explosive. They only needed to be left on the sea bottom underneath a ship to do an amazing amount of damage. As in all other submarines built at this time, she was propelled by an engine which used diesel oil on the surface and storage batteries underwater.

The weeks following the launching were busy for the X3. All the usual surface and underwater trials had to be completed before she was proved satisfactory. The first training class of X-craft submarines began in Northumberland but, like the charioteers, they were soon transferred to Scotland. Secrecy was very important and the submariners, of whom there were now twenty-two, were kept from all contact with the world outside their base. Trials and manoeuvres were held at night and the X3 herself was hidden inside a catamaran.

The X-craft crews, like the charioteers, had problems of discomfort but of quite a different sort. Living in an X-craft was like living in a closed cupboard with two other people. The only place you could stand upright was under the conning tower. In the rest of the boat every action had to be performed bent double unless you were actually lying down. Even then it was impossible to swing one's arms, let alone a cat, without hitting something.

The midget submariner had to be a jack-of-all-trades. He had to know how to work the hydroplanes, ballast tanks and other diving gear and to be able to operate them all at the same time. He had to be able to use the periscope, for both navigational and spying purposes, to start the engines and repair them when they went wrong and to recharge the batteries. As well as all this he had to cook meals, wash up and keep the boat clean. When missions lasted as long as five days it is surprising that he managed to fit in any sleep.

More X-craft had now been built and their name was changed from the 'Experimental' to the '12th Submarine Flotilla'. By September it was decided that the X-craft crews were ready for their shot at the mighty *Tirpitz*. At that time the British had information that besides the 40,000-ton *Tirpitz*, two other prizes were sheltering in the same fiord. These were the 26,000-ton pocket-battleship *Scharnhorst* and the 12,000-ton pocket-battleship *Lützow*. To damage at least one of them could make a difference to the outcome of the war.

On September 11th, six submarines left for Norway, each towing one X-craft on a nylon towrope. They looked a formidable group as they plunged into the North Sea, certainly a more frightening sight than the poor *Arthur* must have looked when setting out on the same mission. Both large and small submarines submerged during the day but at night the large submarines travelled on the surface. The midgets only came up for air when it was absolutely necessary in case they were spotted by the enemy.

The journey of 1,500 miles was eight hard days and nights for the crews of the X-craft. There was so much to do to keep the little submarines going on the long journey that only one person was allowed to sleep at a time. And in spite of all their efforts, the trip was not exactly smooth! The towline between the X8 and her mother submarine *Seanymph* snapped. The big submarine carried on without realizing her loss, and X8 went on alone and eventually found X7 and her mother submarine *Stubborn* who had also become separated by a broken towline. The three of them pressed on together, hoping to catch up with *Seanymph*, but as X8 had no one to tow her through the rough seas she soon got lost again. In the meantime, *Seanymph* had by now noticed her loss, and spent fourteen hours searching in the sea before she finally found the X8 again.

The crew men were exhausted by this time, so a new crew was put on board whilst the others had a long sleep on the *Seanymph*. Once more they were on their way to Norway. Soon after setting off again the unlucky X8 developed a dangerous fault in her explosives. The captain decided to have them dropped in the sea. This was done and they all made off at high speed. It was obviously a fortunate decision: when the submarines were three and a half miles away, the bombs went off with surprising force. Despite the distance between X8 and the explosion she was very nearly wrecked and, after rescuing the crew, she had to be scuttled. Now there were five.

The *Syrtis*, some way in front, also found her towline

had broken from the X9. No amount of searching ever found the poor X9 and she has never been heard of from that day to this.

The four remaining X-craft crossed the sea safely and during the evening of the 20th they left the protection of their parent submarines and struck out alone up the main fiord towards the pride of the German Navy. The *Tirpitz* was anchored in a quiet spot just round a bend at the top of the main Altenfiord in a tiny fiord called Kaafiord. As the X-craft crept slowly on their way the big submarines slipped underwater to wait hopefully for their return.

The midget submarines set off at 8 PM on September 20th. From this moment they had no contact with each other at all. It was a very busy fiord and they had difficulty avoiding the many ships that were travelling up and down it. The X10 began to develop minor defects almost as soon as she was alone. Despite several hours spent on the surface trying to repair them, her condition grew gradually worse as she neared her destination. She was to attack the *Scharnhorst* and the whole crew were looking forward to it! However she became more and more difficult to control; she started hopping up and down in the water like a frog, and water seeped in, causing all the fuses to blow up so that fire extinguishers had to be used.

After they had surfaced to clear the smoke the crew realized that the X10 was too badly damaged to be able to attack the *Scharnhorst* and that they would be very lucky to get home alive. It was 2.15 AM and the X10 was only four and a half miles away from her target. Back on the bottom a very disappointed crew made a start on the very long list of internal repairs that were needed.

The other three boats, X5, X6 and X7 had slipped up the fiord without mishap. Led by the X6 under the command of Lieutenant Donald Cameron, they converged upon the mighty German battleship like ants upon an elephant. The first submarine to arrive at the nets was the X6 which was working very well apart from a flooded periscope which made her almost blind. Cameron was beginning to doubt their chances of getting through the nets without a periscope when they suddenly had a great stroke of luck.

A water-carrying boat with supplies for the *Tirpitz* appeared in front of them and as the nets were opened to admit it, somehow the X6 got whisked in too. To create maximum damage Cameron wanted to lay his charges under the dead centre of the *Tirpitz* but due to his blind periscope he could not do this whilst submerged. Trusting to the luck that had remained with him up to now, he surfaced and in full view of the enemy made his way down half of the *Tirpitz*'s enormous length! The passing of this strange object did not go unnoticed by the sentries up on deck but before they could decide whether it was a machine or a porpoise, Cameron had reached the middle and dived to lay his charges.

By the time he emerged from the other side the Germans had made up their minds and the bullets were really flying. Realizing that escape was impossible and that capture was better than a watery grave, Cameron decided to scuttle the X6 and surrender. The flood valves were opened and as the last of the X6's crew stepped aboard the *Tirpitz* the loyal little submarine sank like a stone. It was then 7.15, one hour before the charges were due to go off.

The X5 got as far as the first set of torpedo nets when she was unfortunately hit by the volley of shots intended for the X6. She must have gone out of control and sunk because that was the last anyone saw of her.

The remaining midget X7, captained by Lieutenant Place, did not have Cameron's luck and had to get through the nets the hard way. After being completely entangled in them twice, Place managed, after an hour of creeping stealthily along the bottom, to bring the midget up only thirty yards from *Tirpitz*. Without hesitating X7 dropped her charges under the vast hull, shot out of the opposite side and back into the anti-torpedo nets like a rabbit into a hole. With their charges set to go off one hour later, not to mention any others which might have been put there first, they didn't want to hang about!

It took forty minutes of charging backwards and forwards through a seemingly endless maze of nets before they found they were free again. Gratefully they submerged to 120 feet and started to put as much distance as possible between themselves and the *Tirpitz*. It was just then that Donald Cameron's hour was up and a mighty explosion shook the whole fiord, tossing the departing X7 up to the surface.

The little submarine, leaking and out of control, was further damaged when the huge guns of the *Tirpitz* opened fire on her. It was obvious that the crew would have to get out quickly if they were to get out at all. As they tried to abandon ship the X7 sank from under them. Place was lucky enough to jump on to a gunnery target but the other three went to the bottom with the damaged X7.

. As the crippled submarine lay there being bombarded by depth charges the three men calmly put on their breathing apparatus and waited until the boat flooded high enough for them to open the hatches. This can only be done when there is equal pressure of water on both sides of the hatch doors, so it was a slow business. Aitken, the ship's diving expert, had taken charge of the team but by the time he got the hatch door open he found that his crewmates were already dead. His own oxygen bottle was also empty and he was very near death himself. As he 'blacked out' he managed to push himself out of the hatch and seconds later was amazed to find himself up on the surface. He and Place were taken on to the *Tirpitz* to join Cameron and his crew.

When the crew of the X6 had been taken on to the *Tirpitz* an hour or so earlier they had been treated with great respect by the Germans who gave them hot coffee and Schnapps and were obviously in the dark about what was to happen to their 'unsinkable' battleship. They had just begun to question the submariners when a series of explosions threw *Tirpitz* six feet into the air.

There was pandemonium on board and the bewildered Germans began shooting in all directions. When the smoke cleared it was surprising to find that the *Tirpitz* was still floating. The crew soon discovered, however, that the large amount of damage would put her out of action for many months, if not for ever. Some months later she did manage to limp down the fiord, only to be set upon immediately by Royal Air Force bomber planes and finally sent down for good.

The six brave survivors, who were well treated and admired for their daring and determination, finally reached prisoner-of-war camps where they stayed until the end of the war. The crew of the X10 were also very lucky. After finishing their repairs they made their way back to the mouth of the fiord where after five harrowing nights of waiting they were picked up by the *Stubborn*.

On September 29th the six parent submarines turned away from Norway and began their return. They were sorry to have only one of the X-craft returning with them but delighted with the success of their joint mission.

Chapter 8

Adventure Under the North Pole

The invention of nuclear power was to make a great difference to the submarine and its place in the world as a powerful weapon. It was also to improve greatly the life of the submariner, giving him safety and comfort to a degree hitherto unknown in the submarine service.

It meant an end to the days of the diesel engine and the sickening smell of its oil that always remained in the forefront of a wartime submariner's memories. It banished the cumbersome storage batteries and the risk of their producing deadly chlorine gas. The bulky oil tanks, that once formed the outer hull of the boat, could now be removed, leaving the submarine with more room inside and a much more streamlined shape.

The absence of diesel engines also meant that there were no more exhaust fumes and tell-tale trails of bubbles that in the past had brought about the death of many a submarine fleeing from the enemy. The nuclear-powered submarine resembled a fish much more closely than had the submarines that had gone before. With her new shape she was faster, more manoeuvrable and absolutely silent. In war she would make a terrifying enemy!

The magic fuel that made possible this vast improvement in every aspect of submarine life was produced by a process called 'nuclear fission'. Nuclear fission takes place within the submarine, inside an enormous steel drum with thick lead walls called a reactor. At the centre of this reactor is a lump of uranium not much bigger than an orange.

The process involves the splitting of atoms of uranium to produce a tremendous amount of heat. The heat is absorbed by water that passes around the uranium and, eventually, after travelling through various sets of pipes at high pressure, it reaches the ship's turbines. Jets of steam from the superheated water drive the turbines, which, in turn, drive the ship's propellers.

Even before World War II the subject of nuclear propulsion had been often talked and written about, but no one had been brave enough to take the plunge into a method so completely untried and, of course, expensive. In 1946 the world's first nuclear reactor was built in Tennessee so that a group of Army, Navy, and civilian people could study nuclear power and how best to use it.

Captain Hyman Rickover, an electrical engineer and submariner, who was put in charge of this experiment, became convinced that nuclear power was the obvious step forward in submarine propulsion. Unfortunately, the US Navy were very doubtful, particularly in view of the vast amount of money needed to produce a submarine of this kind. It took Rickover six years of determined pushing and pleading before the US Navy could be convinced that a nuclear submarine would be a practical weapon.

Finally in June 1952 building was started on a new *Nautilus*. Her reactor was built at a secret place in the desert in Idaho. This was many miles from the boat-building yards of the Electric Boat Company in Connecticut, where the *Nautilus* herself was being built, also in great secrecy. It took nearly two years before she was ready for launching.

She was a large boat displacing 3,180 tons and she was 300 feet long and 38 feet across. Her final cost was thought to be about 55 million dollars and she certainly looked very different from Fulton's *Nautilus*.

Every sailor had his own little cubicle with a comfortable bed instead of the old-fashioned hammock. He had a reading light above it and his own locker. There was a luxurious crew's mess where popular films were regularly shown, and where the seamen could enjoy a TV set, a high-fidelity record-player and an ice-cream and soft-drinks machine. There were three libraries and even an automatic washing machine and spin dryer. Compared with wartime submarines it was a floating hotel!

Unlike previous submarines, she was able to stay submerged for an indefinite period as a result of another invention called a 'carbon-dioxide scrubber'. This was a device that absorbed the poisonous carbon dioxide in the air that the submariners breathed out. Then, when it became necessary, large containers pumped in oxygen to take its place.

On January 21st, 1954, many important people were present to see this wonderful machine launched, among them Rickover, now promoted to Rear-Admiral, and the man who was to be her captain, Commander Wilkinson. It was a typical January day, with a raw coldness and a grey, overcast sky. Yet as Mrs Eisenhower, wife of the United States President, smashed the bottle of champagne on the submarine's bows, the sun magically forced its way through and smiled down on the *Nautilus* and her assembled friends. It was soon to become a traditional saying in the US Submarine Service: 'The sun always shines on the *Nautilus*'.

The submarine moved silently away from the pier, huge and menacing. The sunshine glinted on her conning tower showing her number 571 printed clearly in white against the rest of her black hull. Commander Wilkinson signalled a historic message: 'Under way on nuclear power!'

Nautilus sailed through her trials with ease, breaking every submarine record that had ever existed. Four months after her launching she travelled from New London, Connecticut, to San Juan, Puerto Rico, a distance of 1,381 miles in less than ninety hours. This was ten times farther than any other submarine had travelled without coming to the surface.

The two years following the launching were packed with success for *Nautilus*. She had the distinction of being the only nuclear-powered vehicle in the world and her incredible voyages amazed the world. Everywhere she docked people flocked to catch a glimpse of her.

Ever since the submarine first proved itself as a successful underwater vessel, men have talked of travelling under the ice of the North Pole. The Polar ice cap has always been an object of fascination. It is made up of many miles of packed ice and in these Arctic temperatures only walruses and seals survive. The mystery of what lies beneath its frozen seas has tantalized man for centuries.

To sail under this unfriendly wasteland would be like climbing Mount Everest or landing on the moon – a challenge that could not be ignored although it seemed impossible. Before the days of nuclear power, submarines had attempted to pass under it, taking with them picks and saws to cut their way up to the surface, but even the most daring had only ventured a few miles under the ice.

When the *Nautilus*, the new underwater wonder, showed her amazing capabilities, it seemed obvious that the challenge of the ice-bound seas would be the next test. In spite of this, the plans for *Nautilus'* Polar attempt were labelled top secret. Like the missions of the U-47 and the *Scire*, even the crews were not told about it until they were far out to sea.

A new captain, Commander Anderson, took over *Nautilus* in June 1957 and for the following month *Nautilus* underwent a very thorough overhaul. Engineers installed a gyrocompass, the only sort of compass that works properly near the North Pole. Dr Waldo Lyon came aboard to install his latest invention, the ice fathometer. This clever instrument could measure the distance between the submarine and the ice floating above her and so help her to avoid hitting it.

In August 1957 *Nautilus* set off on her first Polar voyage. As soon as she was out to sea, the *Nautilus* submerged and Anderson told the crew their destination. He was relieved to find them all quite happy about it but he was rather alarmed when he discovered that the main periscope had sprung a leak. Despite this, *Nautilus* made her first dive under the ice at 8 PM on September 7th. After travelling under the ice for quite a distance, the fathometer showed that there was a stretch of clear water directly above them. When the submarine attempted to surface, however, it was brought to a violent halt when it crashed into a thick layer of ice, badly damaging the two periscopes. Clearly, the fathometer was not working properly.

After returning the way they had come, they surfaced in open water to examine the damage. Number 2 periscope was crushed beyond repair and No 1 was badly bent and cracked. Anderson decided that the mission would have to be called off but his engineers had other ideas. In the teeth of a 30-mile-an-hour gale and with the temperature at freezing point, they bent No 1 periscope back to its correct angle and welded together the crack that had formed as a result of the bending. The whole repair, undertaken in the worst possible weather conditions, took fifteen hours.

At 8 AM the next day, with one periscope working, *Nautilus* dipped under the ice again to begin the 660-mile trip to the North Pole. Things went more smoothly this time and the *Nautilus* swiftly and silently penetrated deep under the thick crust of ice that covers the top of the world. She was only 120 miles from the Pole itself when suddenly one of the fuses blew out and both the gyrocompasses stopped working. Without their help it was impossible for the navigator to find his way so Anderson reluctantly gave the order to turn back.

The return journey was not such a happy one for the officers in charge. Working without the valuable gyrocompasses it was easy to imagine *Nautilus* taking the wrong turn and becoming stuck like a steel bubble in an ice cube, completely unable to help herself. They surfaced safely two days later, south of the ice pack. The only consolation was that they had travelled farther north than any other ship, but they were still very disappointed!

A year passed before a further Arctic expedition was arranged for *Nautilus*. This time the submarine would attempt to travel from the Pacific to the Atlantic, crossing the North Pole on the way. She was to be joined in her attempt by another recently built nuclear submarine, the USS *Skate*. They were to approach it by different routes and at different times so there was quite a bit of competitive spirit amongst the two crews. To be the first submarine to cross the Arctic Circle would be a very great achievement indeed!

During the previous winter *Nautilus* had been fitted out with more up-to-date equipment, better fire-fighting apparatus, new gyrocompasses and a television system which transmitted pictures of the ice down into the submarine. A steel collar was also built around her periscopes to prevent any possibility of ice damaging them again.

After this *Nautilus* sailed from the Electric Boat Yard at Groton to Seattle where she was to make the final preparations for her mission. This short trip was to prove almost disastrous as many unexpected faults occurred, some of which were rather serious. The worst setback was a fire in the engine rooms which forced the *Nautilus* to surface in order to use her fire extinguishers. As they gave out poisonous carbon-dioxide fumes, it would have been very dangerous to use them whilst submerged. Had the *Nautilus* been already under the ice cap, there would have been no chance of her coming to the surface. It was a reminder to everyone of the dangers that still existed when working aboard submarines, even one as wonderful as *Nautilus*.

Nautilus left Seattle for the Pole on June 9th. Her crew, including Anderson, were quieter than usual. Even though all the defects had been put right they were still feeling uneasy about the Polar attempt. Their fears were confirmed when only five days later they ran into thick ice many miles farther south than it should have been. It was considered another ill-omen when the new gyrocompass broke down, filling the boat with an air of impending doom. It was not surprising, then, that one depressed sailor thought he spotted a Russian submarine following them. It turned out to be a floating log! By June 18th the ice became so thick that it was impossible to go on so Anderson turned back again and this time anchored at Pearl Harbor.

The next attempt was July 23rd, 1958, by which time all the submarine's faults had been corrected again. *Nautilus* found clear ice-free seas for many miles farther than her last attempt and by July 30th she was ready to submerge for her final run to the Pole. Just before this last dive Anderson found a chunk of ice on *Nautilus'* deck. Impulsively he picked it up, thinking that it might be lucky, and put it into the ship's deep-freeze cabinet.

With the last dive *Nautilus*, the man-made miracle, finally came into her own. Hour after hour, straight as an arrow, she churned through the unknown seas showing to the men, comfortable and warm in 70-degree temperatures, television pictures of the dreaded ice pack constantly moving above them. Instead of being frightening, as they had imagined, it seemed almost beautiful as they carried out their normal routine, eating and sleeping beneath its protective cover.

The *Nautilus*, travelling at twenty knots, ate up mile after mile, creeping deeper and deeper under the crust of ice. As they neared the pole, there was a great feeling of tension and excitement aboard the submarine. Even Commander Anderson was affected. At 11.15 on August 3rd, Anderson was able to tell his crew that they were the first vessel of any sort ever to reach the North Pole! This called for a great celebration which the crew called the 'North Pole Party', and which included someone dressed as 'Santa Claus' who, after all, is the only person supposed actually to live at the North Pole!

The journey back south continued just as smoothly and on August 5th, after spending ninety-six hours, and travelling 1,830 miles, under the ice, the *Nautilus* surfaced in clear water and sunshine. The secrecy was now at an end and the radio operator transmitted the first news of *Nautilus'* successful voyage under the Pole. She sailed on to Iceland where Anderson left the ship and flew over to Washington by helicopter.

Congratulations were sent to *Nautilus* from all over the world. Even the crew of the *Skate* who had been desperately hoping that they would be the first ship to complete this mission hid their disappointment and signalled their good wishes to the triumphant *Nautilus*. Commander Anderson was given what is called a 'citation' from the US President, the only one ever given to a captain of a US ship in peacetime. It praised the historic achievements of the *Nautilus* and described her officers and crew as 'men of skill, professional competency and courage'.

The captain was very proud and in return he presented President and Mrs Eisenhower with one of the ship's clocks that had been stopped at the exact time that they crossed the Pole. Nor did he forget Admiral Rickover, the determined man who had made all this

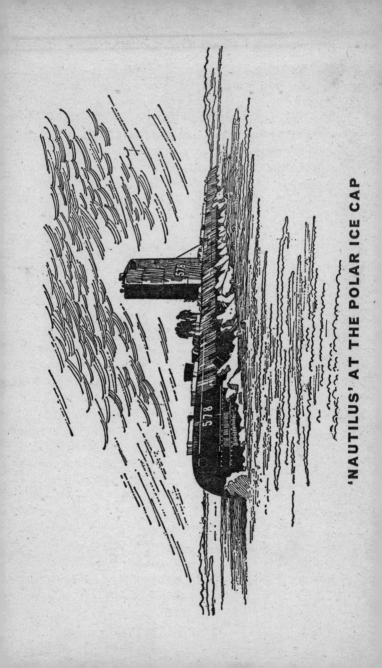

'NAUTILUS' AT THE POLAR ICE CAP

possible. He presented him with the block of Arctic ice that had been kept frozen all the time in the ship's deep freeze!

He then flew back by helicopter to join his ship which was by this time near England and took her back to her birthplace in Connecticut to complete the most amazing voyage in the history of the sea.

More Piccolo Books

A Dictionary of Monsters and Mysterious Beasts 30p
Carey Miller

Everyone is fascinated by monsters: mythical ones like the Minotaur or Werewolf, real ones like Tyrannosaurus Rex, just plain mysterious ones like the Abominable Snowman, or fictional ones like King Kong. An encyclopedic book of nearly 100 stories of strange beasts, with line drawings throughout.

Airships and Balloons 35p
Carey Miller

Amazing tales of airships and balloons, from the one-man hot-air balloons of the 18th century to the huge hydrogen-filled Zeppelins of World War 1.

First Feats 30p
Peter Tunstall

Lindberg, Hillary, Magellan, Bell, Leonov – these men all achieved 'firsts' in their chosen field. 47 exciting stories are told in this lively anthology.

Secrets of the Gypsies 25p
Kay Henwood

A lively account of the customs, rituals and magic of the Romany gypsy, that will fascinate children of eight and over.

Piccolo Picture Histories

Accurate and lavishly illustrated records of man's ingenuity and scientific achievement through the ages, including:

Motor Cars 50p
Colin Munro

The rapid advances in motor-car design and performance from the Catley and Ayes Steam Wagonette of 1868 to the Ferrari P4 racing/sports cars of today.

Aircraft 50p
Maurice Allward

How aircraft have developed from the Wright Brothers' *Flyer 1* to the supersonic *Concorde* which is taking aviation to the limits of present-day techniques.

Locomotives 50p
Brian Reed

The majestic progress of the locomotive from Blenkinsop's Rack Engines of 1812 to RENFE diesel-hydraulics and French quadri-current electrics.

Ships 50p
Laurence Dunn

The absorbing story of ships through the ages from Egyptian boats of papyrus reeds to the famous HMS *Ark Royal*, recommissioned in 1970 at a cost of 30 million pounds.

A Diary of Yesterdays 45p
Tony Bastable

You will enjoy looking through this unusual diary, which contains a day-by-day record of anniversaries both modern and centuries old. There are entries for each of the 365 days and some surprising 'birthdays' come to light.

A Piccolo original in association with Thames Television – Magpie

Piccolo All The Year Round Book 50p
Deborah Manley

For each month of the year, a wealth of ideas for things to make and do, facts about weather and history, famous birthdays, seasonal poems and much more. A superb 'year book' to dip into throughout the twelve months.

Piccolo Book of Everyday Inventions 50p
Meredith Hooper

How were the cornflake, the typewriter, chewing gum or Coca-cola first invented? The stories behind these and many other indispensable items of our everyday life are vividly described in this excellently written and lively book.

You can buy these and other Piccolo books from booksellers and newsagents; or direct from the following address:
Pan Books, Cavaye Place, London SW10 9PG
Send purchase price plus 15p for the first book and 5p for each additional book, to allow for postage and packing

While every effort is made to keep prices low, it is sometimes necessary to increase prices at short notice. Pan Books reserve the right to show on covers new retail prices which may differ from those advertised in the text or elsewhere